AMBERGRIS CAYE
COVID RELIEF
COOKBOOK

*100% of Profits Donated
to Feed Those in Need*

CREATED THANKS TO THE
GENEROSITY OF
AMBERGRIS CAYE
RESTAURANTS, CHEFS,
RESIDENTS
AND VISITORS

Foreword by Kimberly Wylie

CYPRESS CANYON PUBLISHING

COPYRIGHT

Cypress Canyon Publishing

Dedication

This book is dedicated to all of the amazing people of Ambergris Caye.

Together, we will overcome this.

#SanPedroStrong

Photo by Olivera Rusu

Foreword

I first came to Ambergris Caye in 2009 and immediately fell in love. How could you not love this island? The only thing warmer than the soft, sandy beaches and crystal clear turquoise waters is the hearts of the Belizean people.

This is an island where strangers quickly become friends and friends eventually become family.

I have numerous stories of the generosity, the honesty and the kindness of San Pedranos. From a musician who helped us late at night fix our headlights on our golf cart with a guitar string to a gentleman who saw my windblown $20 bill under my golf cart and stopped me to give it back to me.

One of my now good friends, Frankel "Mac" Logan, owner of Enell's Grill, trusted me with a cheeseburger and fries, when I had no cash on hand. His "No problem. Pay me later." response was mind-boggling to me at the time. I could not fathom walking into a restaurant in the United States and having them offer to make me food, even if I didn't have money on me.

But this is the Belizean people.

They are trusting. As I sat with Mac while my burger was being made he told me, "Most people, they're good people. The ones that aren't – I leave that to Karma."

This is Belize. The real Belize.

Good-hearted people you meet one time and are immediately invited to a family barbecue that weekend. They are the people you give a ride to on the side of the road and end up spending the whole afternoon picking "Caye Caulkers" – coco plums – with. They wave to strangers as they pass. They are happy to strike up a conversation with you. They are our friend, Damien, on the bridge who always greets us with a smile, a fist bump, and a "Have a great day!"

These are people who may not have much materialistically, but they are so much richer than so many others for it. Their kids play outside kicking a soccer ball around or goofing off in the ocean. They work hard for their money – really, really hard. And they enjoy life just as hard. I have learned so much from my Belizean family, and my life is so much better for having them in it.

And now they need our help.

The COVID19 virus has crippled the world. It has done untold damage to our physical health, our mental health and our financial health. But here on Isla Bonita, the damage is almost beyond measure.

Ambergris Caye's only industry is tourism.

Coming off an incredibly short and slow "high season" many of our businesses, and their employees, were already struggling. With our first Coronavirus case on March 23, the island was put on complete quarantine. This was coupled with the closing of the only international airport, in Belize City, the Philip Goldson International Airport.

Tourism was instantly and completely gone.

For the first several weeks, the only businesses allowed open, other than medical facilities, were grocery stores, tortillerias, and produce stands. Restaurants and hotels and tour operators, the lifeblood of our little island, were forced to close. Overnight thousands of people were unemployed – people who were already struggling and who had so little to start with.

To make matters worse, by government mandate, fishing was prohibited.

We instantly had a large number of people who could no longer feed themselves.

Quickly, people started to step up to help their friends and neighbors – their island families. Hope Haven, a long time resource for those in need on the island sprang into action. Cultural groups, including the Muslim and Chinese communities came together to donate food. Churches and individuals came forward to offer clean drinking water for families, as without income not only could people not buy food, but they couldn't purchase potable water either.

And then Maresha Reid came forward.

Maresha Reid is the owner of Pirate's Treasure Restaurant and Bar, which features her amazing Chef's Table where Maresha whips up an incredible, multi-course meal, around an open hearth, while guests watch. She also owns Pirate's Not-So-Secret Beach Bar & Grill. She saw people struggling to feed themselves and her natural instinct was to feed them. She realized much of the food being donated was shelf-stable items, given many Belizeans do not have refrigeration. And these, as a result, were high sodium, preservative-filled canned goods. She asked – "Wouldn't it be better to provide home-cooked, healthy and nutritious meals to people instead?"

The San Pedro Hot Lunch Program was born!

Now, three times a week, Maresha and her crew of volunteers serve hundreds of hot meals. As of the writing of this book, they are serving approximately 350 meals per day!

But there are so many more people they have to turn away.

This is where this cookbook comes in.

100% of the profits from this book will be donated to the San Pedro Hot Lunch Program, to purchase food and supplies to continue to feed those in need on the island.

Within the covers you will find 96 recipes crafted and kindly contributed by local restaurateurs, chefs, Ambergris Caye residents and Ambergris Caye visitors. You'll find dozens of Belizean dishes and dozens of non-Belizean dishes. At first, I had thought about doing only Belizean dishes. But I quickly realized one of the things I love about this country, and about the island specifically, is it's truly a melting pot of cultures from all over the world. So why not include all of the recipes contributors love so dearly even though they aren't a quintessential "Belizean dish?"

I personally thank you for your purchase of this cookbook. You've helped ensure people on the island didn't go to sleep tonight hungry. You are touching lives you may never meet, but are forever in your debt.

Wishing you and your loved ones all the blessings of health and happiness and hoping you can soon come and visit our little slice of paradise.

Maresha Reia
Founder of San Pedro Hot Lunch

Editor's Note

Please note, due to the urgency of the situation on Ambergris Caye and a desire to start helping people as quickly as possible, this cookbook was put together very quickly. As such, many of the recipes do not have photos accompanying them. In their place, you will find photos of Maresha Reid's Hot Lunch Program and photos of our beautiful island.

This cookbook would not have been possible without the support of the numerous restaurants, chefs, residents, and visitors of Ambergris Caye who contributed recipes. Seeing a community come together so quickly for a cause is not only heart-warming, but awe-inspiring.

I encourage everyone to please visit all of the contributor's establishments, when you have a chance to visit our tiny island. Let them know you too think their contribution was wonderful!

I would like to add a HUGE thank you to all of those who contributed photographs for this book, including:

L. Kelly Jones Photography – KellyJonesPhotography.com

Olivera Rusu – PhotographyInBelize.com

Grant Wylie

Rebecca Coutant author, *Fifty Big Experiences on Ambergris Caye, Belize* and owner of SanPedroScoop.com

Lastly, although we've tried to prevent it, due to the rapid production of this book, there may be typos or errors within the text. If you find any needed corrections, please do not hesitate to contact us at COVIDcookbook@cypresscanyonbooks.com.

Thank you, once again, for your support!

Table of Contents

Photo by L. Kelly Jones

Photo by Olivera Rusu
at Las Terrazas

BELIZEAN

Cuisine

A Word About Belizean Cuisine

Belizean cuisine is primarily influenced by the rich history of the country itself and the people who have come to call it home. You'll find Maya, Kriol, Garifuna, Mestizo and British cultures as the base of the most well-known Belizean foods. Our neighbors, Mexico to the north and Guatemala to the south (especially with their pupusas), have also made their impact on Belizean food. However, other influences, from a wide variety of cultures in far-flung places around the world, including the Mennonites, Chinese and Lebanese, just to name a few, have had their hand in developing an ever-evolving and ever-expanding array of foodie wonders to explore in Belize.

One of the common spice combinations you'll find in Belizean cooking is recado – both in its red form (often referred to simply as recado) and also black recado. Red recado is well worth making yourself, and I've included my recipe for you to use. However, black recado is more difficult to make. It's base is roasted ancho chile peppers. This process produces a lot of smoke. And this smoke is incredibly irritating to the lungs and eyes. If you are not in Belize, Amazon has black recado (recado negro) you can order and have delivered. If you do attempt making it yourself, make sure you do it outside.

The other staple in Belizean cooking is masa dough. You'll find a recipe for this as well, courtesy of Nancy Lindley. This is a corn meal dough used as the base for many dishes, including panades, salbutes tamales, tamalitos, and garnaches.

Photo by Olivera Rusu @ Pelican Reef Villa

BELIZEAN COOKING STAPLES

Recado (Recado Rojo)

Courtesy of Kimberly Wylie

This is one of the more common spice combinations you'll find in Belizean cooking. It's the spice mix that makes Belizean Stewed Chicken so amazing! It's difficult to find, especially outside of Belize, but relatively easy to make.

INGREDIENTS:

2 Tbsp Achiote (Annato) Seeds

½ cup Water

5 cloves Garlic, skins on

½ large White Onions, sliced

1 Tbsp dried Mexican Oregano

1 tsp Cumin

¼ tsp Ground Clove

1 tsp Ground Allspice

⅛ tsp Ground Cinnamon

1 tsp Black Pepper

¼ tsp Ground Cayenne Pepper

½ cup Ancho Chili Powder

1 Tbsp Salt

2 Tbs White Vinegar

1 to 1 ½ cups Orange Juice

INSTRUCTIONS:

1. Simmer achiote seeds in water for 20 minutes. Remove from heat and allow to steep for at least 2 hours to soften.

2. In a dry skillet, toast skin on garlic cloves and onion slices, on low heat, until golden and soft on the inside.

3. In a blender or food processor, blend all ingredients, adding just enough orange juice to make a paste.

4. Store in air tight container in the refrigerator.

Packing food for San Pedro Hot Lunch

TIPS:

- Achiote seeds are a very strong red color. BE CAREFUL – it will stain your clothes and hands!
- You may be able to find achiote (annatto) powder pre-ground. Badia makes it and it's very handy, as you can skip the steeping of the seeds. If you use powder, reduce the amount to 1 ½ Tbsp
- If you are unable to find achiote seeds or powder, you can substitute 1 Tbsp turmeric plus 1 Tbsp sweet paprika to come close.
- If you cannot find Mexican oregano (look in a Hispanic market or specialty food retailer like Whole Foods), you can substitute dried marjoram. In a pinch, you can use standard (Mediterranean) oregano.

Flour Tortillas

Courtesy of "La Miskita" Soguey of Ecologic Divers
EcologicDivers.com

Diving in Ambergris Caye is some of the best diving in the world, with the Meso-American reef right offshore. My favorite dive shop is Ecologic Divers. Their divemasters are super-knowledgeable, friendly and always safety conscious. If you're not a diver, Ecologic has snorkeling excursions, fishing excursions and mainland tours for you to enjoy.

INGREDIENTS:

¼ tsp Baking Soda

¼ tsp Salt

2 Tbsp Shortening

1 lb Flour

1 cup Water...ish

INSTRUCTIONS:

1. Mix all the ingredients together, with just enough water to make a dough.

2. Knead it and then separate into 12 "lumps"

3. Coat hands in shortening and form lumps into balls. Balls should have a thin layer of shortening around them to prevent sticking to each other. Keep track of which was first; this must be first to be cooked.

4. Cover with plastic and wait 15 minutes...no longer or dough will harden too much.

5. Pre-heat a cast iron skillet.

6. Use a press or flatten in hands by slapping between hands (don't flour and roll) until thin - 1/8 inch thickness. They won't be consistent throughout.

7. Cook on cast iron until desired "doneness."

Masa Dough (Corn Dough)

Courtesy of Nancy Lindley

Masa Dough is used in a lot of Belizean dishes including tamales, tamalitos, salbutes, and garnaches.

INGREDIENTS:

1lb Masa

1 tsp Recado (see pg. 20)

1 tsp Baking Powder

½ tsp Salt

1 Tbsp Water

2 Tbsp Coconut Oil

½ tsp Vinegar

Additional water as needed

INSTRUCTIONS:

1. Dissolve recado in water.

2. Mix together masa, baking powder and salt.

3. Add recado to masa mixture.

4. Stir in oil and vinegar.

5. Continue to add more water until you have a dough which is about the consistency of playdough.

Photo by Olivera Rusu

Easy Corn Tortillas

Courtesy of Kimberly Wylie

On Ambergris Caye, we eat corn tortillas with everything. And there are many tortillerias where you can buy them very inexpensively. However, when you're not on island, this recipe will help you enjoy fresh-made tortillas you can make from scratch, at home.

INGREDIENTS:

2 cups Masa Harina

1 ½ to 2 cups Water, very warm

INSTRUCTIONS:

1. Add just enough water to masa to a large mixing bowl to create a dough.

2. Let rest 5 minutes.

3. Knead dough for 5 minutes, until dough is smooth and pliable.

4. Divide dough into 16 pieces and roll each into a ball.

5. If you have a tortilla press, follow the directions of your press. However, if you don't have a press, place a ball between two sheets of wax paper and flatten as much as you can with your hand.

6. Then use a rolling pin to roll out into a circle, turning 90 degrees after each roll, until your tortilla is about 1/16th-inch thick.

7. Cook on a hot skillet for 30 seconds then flip to the other side. Your tortillas should be lightly-toasted and you may see small air pockets form in the dough.

8. Wrap in foil until ready to serve.

BELIZEAN BREAKFASTS

Belizean Stuff(ed) Fry Jack

Courtesy of Chef Bella of PUR Boutique Cabana and Taco Bar

PURBoutiqueCabanas.com

Try these Stuffed Fry Jacks and Ms. Bella's Famous Stew(ed) Red Beans and more at PUR Boutique Cabana & Taco Bar! PUR is located on Ambergris Caye, just 1 mile north of the bridge. This is a wonderful stop for a social afternoon with a swim-up pool bar in one of the only adults-only settings on the island. Plus, they have the best (and the HUGEST) burritos on Ambergris Caye!

FRY JACK DOUGH INGREDIENTS:

2 cups All-Purpose Flour

3 tsp Baking Powder

¼ tsp Salt

1 Tbsp Crisco Shortening, butter flavor

Vegetable oil for frying

1 cup Water

INSTRUCTIONS:

1. Stir flour, baking powder, and salt in a bowl.

2. Cut shortening into flour, add water a little at a time, to make a soft, but not sticky, dough.

3. Cover dough with a pan and leave to rest about 15 to 20 minutes.

4. Cut lengthwise into 2- to 3-in balls, and then cut crosswise to desired size.

5. Heat oil and fry on each side, until fluffy and golden brown.

FILLINGS:

You have the option to serve with cheese, refried beans, eggs of your choice, and/or breakfast meat of your choice. (see picture 1)These are also often served in Belizean homes only with butter, honey or jam.

At PUR - we make one EXTRA large (football-sized!) fry jack, and fill the middle with the breakfast options - and fold over like the picture above.

Nancy's Belizean Fry Jacks

Courtesy of Nancy Lindley

Like many Belizean recipes, each person has their own favorite take on the classics. It's always good to try a variety of variations, to find which you and your family prefer.

INGREDIENTS:

4 cups All-Purpose Flour

1½ tsp Salt

2 tsp Baking Powder

¼ cup Shortening

1 ½ cups Water (use a little more if needed)

Vegetable or Canola Oil for frying

INSTRUCTIONS:

1. Measure flour into a large bowl.

2. Add baking powder and salt and combine.

3. Work shortening into dry ingredients, either with your hands or with a pastry blender, until mixture resembles cornmeal.

4. Make a well in the center of the flour mixture and pour water into the well.

5. Mix until a smooth, slightly sticky dough forms.

6. Knead dough for 5 minutes.

7. Divide dough into 12 balls.

8. Lightly grease the dough balls with shortening.

9. Let dough balls rest for 20 minutes.

10. Lightly grease a sheet of tinfoil

11. Using your fingers spread dough out into a circle on tinfoil and cut in half.

12. Heat approximately 1 to 2 inches of oil in a heavy bottomed frying pan.

13. Place dough in hot oil (it should puff right up).

14. Fry for a few minutes on each side, until golden brown.

TIPS:

- Make sure you have enough oil in your pan (1 inch or more).
- Make sure your oil is hot (medium high heat).
- Don't spread the dough too thin.
- Don't cut a slit in the halves if you want a puffy fry jack.

Belizean Meat Pies

Courtesy of Nancy Lindley

Although these don't sound like a breakfast item, meat pies are one of the most popular breakfast meals on the island. These delicious Belizean staples are a hearty way to start your day and can be found at various food stands, as well as by folks selling them on the street from coolers.

FILLING INGREDIENTS:

1 lb Ground Sirloin	1 tsp Red Recado (see pg. 20)
1 tsp Salt	$1/_3$ cup Green Bell Peppers, diced
½ tsp Ground Black Pepper	¾ cup Onion, diced
½ tsp Thyme	1 to 2 tsp Flour
1 tsp Allspice	¾ cup Water

INSTRUCTIONS:

1. Brown meat and season with salt, black pepper, thyme, allspice, and recado.

2. Fold in onion, bell peppers and garlic until combined.

3. Add ¾ cup water and cook for about 20 minutes, stirring occasionally.

4. Dissolve 1 to 2 teaspoons flour in 2 tablespoons water and add to meat mixture to thicken. Cook approximately 5 minutes or until mixture is thickened but not dry.

6. Set aside.

CRUST INGREDIENTS:

2 cups All-Purpose Flour	½ tsp Salt
5 Tbsp Shortening or Butter	6 to 7 Tbsp Water, cold

INSTRUCTIONS:

1. Measure flour and salt into a large bowl and stir to combine all ingredients.

2. Cut fat into dry ingredients with a pastry blender until it resembles small peas.

3. Sprinkle cold water over dry ingredients slowly, stirring with a fork to distribute, until the dough just comes together.

4. Roll out to ⅛-inch thickness.

ASSEMBLY:

1. Preheat oven to 350°F.
2. Cut 5 ½-inch circles out of crust to line 18 muffin tins with crust.
3. Add one heaping tablespoon of filling to each pastry.
4. Top with 2 ¼-inch circle of pastry crust, and fold over edges to seal.
5. Bake at for approximately 25 minutes.

Packing food for San Pedro Hot Lunch

Best One Bowl Made for Belize Banana Bread

Courtesy of Rebecca Coutant – Author of *Fifty Big Experiences in Ambergris Caye, Belize*
SanPedroScoop.com

A note from Rebecca:

I'm not a big cook but I always LOVED baking when I lived in the States. I love the precision – the order of it all. If you follow the directions, you are bound to get something delicious.

But when I moved to Ambergris Caye 13 years ago, I realized there were SO many additional factors to consider – like ingredients. Imported chocolate chips and butter are 2 to 4 times as expensive in Belize as they are in the US. Many ingredients common in desserts (like berries or nuts or heavy cream) are even more expensive or not available at all. Throw in the fact the temperature here hovers around 80 degrees year-round...it's not exactly the ideal climate for firing up your oven.

So I wanted a recipe that was easy and delicious, enjoyed by Belizeans and visitors alike, and used easy to find, very affordable ingredients. Bananas are available year-round, grown in abundance here and affordable! Anywhere from 4 to 10 for $1 BZD, depending on the part of the country you live in.

I played around with all sorts of versions of banana bread to get to this place. I tried expensive butter (all butter is expensive in Belize); I tried milk or Greek yogurt; I tried different flours. And I found the most simple IS also the most moist, most banana-y and my favorite. ALL ingredients are easy and affordable in Belize, and if you want to jazz it up (I suggest with mini-chocolate chips or the crumble), it's just more delicious.

INGREDIENTS:

3 medium to large Bananas, as ripe as possible (or just defrost those oldies but goodies you have in the freezer)

½ cup Vegetable Oil (not coconut oil)

1 cup Sugar (white or brown)

2 Eggs

1 tsp Vanilla (rum also works)

1 ½ cups Flour

1 tsp Baking Soda

¾ tsp Salt

1 tsp Cinnamon

Photo courtesy of Rebecca Coutant author Fifty Big Experiences on Ambergris Caye, Belize
SanPedroScoop.com

INSTRUCTIONS:

1. Preheat oven to 325° F.

2. In a large bowl, smash the bananas until mostly smooth. (Small lumps fine)

3. Add the vegetable oil and the sugar. Mix until blended.

4. Add the eggs and vanilla. Again mix until blended.

5. Add flour, baking soda (make sure there are no lumps in your dry ingredients...just crush with your fingers if there are), cinnamon and salt on top of wet mixture. Mix all until just blended.

6. Oil your baking pan(s) liberally. You can use one large loaf pan or smaller loaf pans. I always use 3 mini-loaf pans (5 ¾" by 3 1/4 by 2 ¼") - because I like to give the bread away.

7. Pour batter evenly into pans. Bake until the bread is peanut butter brown and firm at the peak. When you stick a fork or cake tester in to the highest point, the tester will come out clean. My 3 mini-loaves take 45-50 minutes in my small convection oven at 325° F.

8. Remove loaves from oven, cool 10 minutes and remove from pans to rack to cool. It is always tempting to cut when hot, but it's not worth it. It just doesn't taste as good.

9. Store in a closed container for up to 2 days (in Belize heat)...probably a few more days in more temperate climates. If you plan on eating them later, they freeze BEAUTIFULLY for up to a few months.

CRUMBLE OPTION INGREDIENTS:

5 Tbsp Oats (quick or old fashioned)

5 Tbsp Flour

3 Tbsp Sugar

2 Tbsp Butter, cold

¼ tsp Cinnamon

Photo courtesy of Rebecca Coutant

CRUMBLE OPTION INSTRUCTIONS:

1. If you are adding crumble: In a small bowl, mix the butter and dry ingredients together for the crumb. It's easiest to use a fork or your fingers to smush the butter in evenly...so that the mixture becomes a course crumb.

2. After you pour the batter into your loaf pan(s), sprinkle crumble topping on top and bake per the normal instructions.

TIP:

- Additionally, you can add any of all of the following: chocolate chips (I find the minis work best), shredded coconut, walnuts, a few schmears of Nutella (fill you loaf pan half way with batter, spread some Nutella, and then cover with batter)

Johnny Cakes

Courtesy of Kimberly Wylie

Flatter than biscuits and heartier than English muffins, Johnny Cakes are a great start to any day. Some people eat them with just butter. I've heard of others putting cheese on them. I like mine drizzled with honey and sometimes spread with peanut butter. A little jam is also nice.

INGREDIENTS:

3 cups Flour

½ tsp Salt

2 tsp Baking Powder

5 Tbsp Sugar

¼ cup Unsalted Butter, softened

1 (12 oz) can Coconut Milk

Photo by Grant Wylie

INSTRUCTIONS:

1. Preheat oven to 350° F.

2. In a bowl, mix together flour, salt, baking powder and sugar.

3. Cut in butter into dry ingredients.

4. Add just enough coconut milk to create a shaggy dough. Begin to knead to bring dough together. Continue to knead for a couple of minutes, until flour is well-incorporated. Do not overwork, because you don't want tough Johnny Cakes.

5. Cut dough into 10 equal pieces and roll into nice, smooth balls.

6. Place on cookie sheet, with at least 1-inch of spacing between them, and slightly flatten so each dough ball is an approximately ¼-inch thick disc.

7. Gently poke each disc several times with a fork, going about halfway into the disc.

8. Bake for 25 minutes, on the middle rack, then leaving the sheet in the middle position, turn your broiler on to High and broil for 2 minutes, until tops are golden brown.

9. Slice and serve with your favorite topping.

Belizean Breakfast

Courtesy of Kimberly Wylie

Serves 4

Belizean breakfast varies depending on where you get it, with each cook doing it a little bit differently. This is my version.

INGREDIENTS:

6 Eggs

2 Tbsp Unsalted Butter

1 Tomato, finely diced

½ Green Pepper, finely diced

½ White Onion, finely diced

Salt and Pepper to taste

INSTRUCTIONS:

1. Heat skillet on medium high heat and add butter.

2. Add tomato, green pepper and onion to the skillet and cook until soft.

3. Add eggs and reduce heat to medium.

4. Stir constantly until scrambled to your desired consistency and season to taste.

Serve with:

- Fry Jacks (see pg. 27)
- Refried Beans (see pg. 52)
- Ham or Bacon

TIP:

Top your eggs and beans with a little Marie Sharp's hot sauce for an authentic Belizean breakfast! (You can get it on Amazon.com while you wait for your trip to Ambergris Caye.)

Photo by Olivera Rusu at Pelican Reef Villas

Photo by Olivera Rusu

BELIZEAN APPPETIZERS

Pirate's Caribbean Shrimp Ceviche

Courtesy of Maresha Reid of Pirate's Treasure & Pirate's Secret Beach
Facebook.com/PiratesTreasureRestaurantAndBar

Pirate's Treasure is located ½ mile north of the bridge. Pirate's Treasure combines a fun and lively bar, with yummy bar bites, with Maresha's Chef's Table – an amazing, personalized culinary experience, where Maresha whips up a multi-course meal, on an open hearth, right before your eyes!

Her second location – Pirate's Secret Beach – is the ultimate Secret Beach destination. Once you get to the Secret Beach area, just keep going straight and park. You'll find lots of loungers, with lots of shade. Tons of in-water tables are available for noshing on the best food in the Secret Beach area.

INGREDIENTS:

10 large Raw Shrimp, peeled and deveined

1 large Tomato, deseeded and thinly julienned

¼ Red Onion, thinly julienned

¼ cup Cilantro, roughly chopped not super fine

2 to 3 Limes, juiced

1 Tbsp Seasoned Salt

1 tsp Black Pepper, coarsely ground

½ tsp Chile Molido/Ground Habanero (substitute with 1/4 tsp Cayenne and ¼ tsp Paprika)

INSTRUCTIONS:

1. To prepare shrimp, bring a small pot of water to boil and cook shrimp for 2 to 3 minutes, then blanch by removing and place in a bowl of ice water for another 2 minutes.

2. Once cooled, chop each shrimp into 3 to 4 pieces, place in a mixing bowl and squeeze lime juice evenly over all shrimp. Choose a bowl that will be able to fit and can be stirred with all other ingredients included.

3. Add a splash of water allowing all shrimp to be submerged at least half way and set aside.

4. Proceed to prepare tomato, onions and cilantro. Toss into bowl of marinated shrimp, sprinkle all spices and mix together.

5. Taste and adjust spices for your preference of heat and balance. Add lime juice for tartness and serve with chips.

TIP:

- You may add small diced cucumbers and carrots for an even more vibrant summer finish!

Conch Ceviche

Courtesy of Kimberly Wylie

This ceviche recipe is a variation of the one I learned the very first time we were in Belize. We had stayed at a few places that trip, so we could get a feel for the different parts of the island, including a couple of nights at Captain Morgan's. While there, they had a "ceviche class" at their swim-up bar. I had never had ceviche before, nor had I made it, and this little impromptu (and free!) class was a game changer. Over the last decade, I've tweaked my recipe from what I recalled from that class. (Many drinks made it difficult to remember the ingredients exactly that day.) I love to serve this in a clean conch shell with lots of fresh tortilla chips.

INGREDIENTS:

1 lb Conch Meat, finely diced

12 Tbsp Lime Juice

1 lb Tomatoes

½ lb Red Onion

½ bunch Cilantro Leaves

½ to 1 Jalapeno to taste (seeded and deveined if you don't like spicy)

½ Avocado

Salt and Black Pepper to taste

Tortilla Chips

Photo by Olivera Rusu

INSTRUCTIONS:

1. Finely dice conch meat and place in a glass bowl with the lime juice. Allow to sit for at least 15 minutes. This acid chemically "cooks" the meat.

2. Dice tomatoes, onions and avocado and Roughly chop the cilantro leaves.

3. Finely dice (and seed and devein, if you prefer) the jalapeno.

4. Once conch is marinated for at least 15 minutes, add veggies to the bowl and stir.

5. Season with salt and pepper to taste and serve with tortilla chips.

TIPS:

- Adding a little fresh pineapple or mango diced up to this dish is a fun twist!
- Instead of conch, or in addition, you can use shrimp, lobster, or a variety of saltwater fish.

Shrimp Ceviche

Courtesy of Hidden Treasure

HiddenTreasureBelize.com

Serves 2

If you're looking for elegant, fine dining on Ambergris Caye - Hidden Treasure is where you need to be. This award-winning restaurant is tucked into the Escalante neighborhood, and truly is a hidden treasure! There is nothing more romantic than dining by candlelight, in rustic, but elegantly-appointed surroundings. Hidden Treasure is on my "must go" list when we have friends and family visiting.

INGREDIENTS:

1 lb Shrimp, cleaned & deveined
    & chopped

½ cup Lime Juice

Salt & Black Pepper (to taste)

1 large Onion, chopped

1 large Tomato, chopped

Fresh Cilantro, finely chopped

1 Cucumber, chopped

1 Habanero Pepper, chopped
    (optional)

Tortilla Chips

Photo courtesy of Hidden Treasure

INSTRUCTIONS:

1. In one big bowl, put the fresh chopped shrimp (or seafood of your choice) and pour in the ½-cup lime juice.

2. Add salt and pepper to taste.

3. Add onion, tomato, cilantro, cucumber, and habanero if using.

4. Stir to combine and serve with tortilla chips.

Belizean Cheese Dip

Courtesy of Kimberly Wylie

Belizean cheese dip is usually served cold, but if you'd like, you can microwave it to warm it up. I won't tell anyone.

INGREDIENTS:

1 pound Happy Cow Cheese – cut into chunks

½ White Onion – cut into chunks

1 can (7 oz) Salsa Casera

½ bunch Cilantro – leaves only

½ Jalapeno Pepper (veined and seeded if you don't like spicy)

½ to 1 can (12 oz) Evaporated Milk

INSTRUCTIONS:

1. Place all ingredients, including half of the can of evaporated milk, into the blender.

2. Blend until ingredients start to become smooth.

3. Add more evaporated milk, as needed, to make mixture dip-like consistency.

4. Serve with tortilla chips and enjoy!

TIP:

* This dip can be refrigerated for up to a week, in an air-tight container.

Photo by Grant Wylie

Rockin' Seafood Dip

Courtesy of Aleta Hidinger

INGREDIENTS:

½ lb Shrimp/Crab, picked & cleaned

1 (8 oz.) package Cream Cheese

½ cup Sour Cream

2 Tbsp Mayonnaise

1 Tbsp Lemon Juice

1 tsp Worcestershire Sauce

½ tsp Dry Mustard

1 Tbsp Milk

¼ cup Cheddar Cheese, grated

½ tsp Garlic Salt

INSTRUCTIONS:

1. Preheat oven to 325° F.

2. Mix cream cheese, mayo, sour cream, lemon juice, Worcestershire sauce, mustard and garlic salt in a bowl.

3. Add enough milk to make a creamy consistency, then stir in half of the cheddar cheese and all the seafood.

Lots of food for the San Pedro Hot Lunch Program

4. Pour into 1 quart casserole dish and top with remaining cheese.

5. Bake for 30 minutes until mixture is bubbly and brown on top.

6. Garnish with paprika (optional) and serve with crackers or chips!

Coconut Bean Garnache

Courtesy of Kieron Lennan a Red Seal Chef who lives in San Pedro, Belize

Garnaches are a traditional dish composed of fried corn tortillas topped with refried beans, shredded cabbage, cheese, and other garnishes. Garnaches are especially popular in Belize, being available in most restaurants as a common appetizer.

INGREDIENTS:

Masa Dough (see pg. 22)

Refried Beans (see pg. 52)

Cooking Oil

¼ lb of Dutch Grated Cheese (Edam)

INSTRUCTIONS:

1. Roll 1 inch masa dough, press dough to form circle $\frac{1}{8}$-inch thick.

2. Heat oil over medium heat until hot.

3. Fry dough until golden brown.

4. Remove and drain well on paper towels.

3. Spread refried beans onto fried tortilla.

4. Sprinkle with cheese and enjoy!

Photo by Olivera Rusu

Conch Fritters

Courtesy of Kimberly Wylie

INGREDIENTS:

½ lb Conch Meat

2 tsp Garlic Powder

1 tsp Chicken Bouillon

½ White Onion, minced

½ Red Pepper, minced

2 Tbsp Cilantro Leaves, minced

1 tsp Jalapeno, minced

1 tsp Baking Powder

1 tsp Salt

1 ½ cups Water

3 cups Flour

Vegetable Oil

INSTRUCTIONS:

1. Heat vegetable oil in large pot.

2. Mix conch, garlic powder, bouillon, onion, pepper, cilantro, jalapeno, baking powder, salt, and water.

3. Add enough flour to make a thick batter.

4. Place large spoonfuls of dough in oil and cook until golden brown, turning as necessary.

5. Remove from oil and drain on paper towels

Jicama and Mango with Chile & Lime

Courtesy of Kimberly Wylie

As I write this book, it's mango season on the island! It's my favorite time of year, because there's nothing better than a fresh mango on a hot day —juicy and sweet. This is a simple and healthy appetizer that can be put together in only a few minutes.

INGREDIENTS:

1 Jicama

3 Mangoes

2 Limes, juiced

1 tsp Chili Powder

INSTRUCTIONS:

1. Peel and slice the jicama into strips.

2. Remove the flesh from the mango cheeks and cut those into strips.

3. Mix the jicama and mango in a bowl with the lime juice.

4. Sprinkle the chili powder over the fruit and serve.

TIP:

- To remove the flesh easily from a mango, use a drinking glass! First, run your knife through the mango, along the wide, flat edge of the mango pit. This is the "cheek" of the mango. Then to remove the skin, slide the cheek along the far edge of a drinking glass, pushing away from you, to separate the mango skin from the flesh.

BELIZEAN SOUPS, SALADS, & SIDE DISHES

Escabeche

Courtesy of Patty Velez

INGREDIENTS:

2 lb Boneless Chicken (parts or breasts)

1 tsp Lemon Pepper

2 Tbsp Canola Oil or Avocado Oil

2 Tbsp Chicken Bouillon Granules

2 Tbsp Pickled Jalapeño Juice

2 Tbsp Apple Cider Vinegar

½ tsp Mexican Oregano

1 clove Garlic, peeled and minced

1 cup Carrots, thinly sliced

3 White Onions, sliced into thin rings

7 cups of Water – divided

Cilantro – chopped for garnish

Lime – sliced for garnish

INSTRUCTIONS:

1. Cut chicken into bite-sized pieces.

2. In hot oil cook chicken, seasoned only with lemon pepper, until golden on each side (approximately 4-5 minutes each side).

3. Set aside.

4. In a stockpot, bring 5 cups of water to boil.

5. Add bouillon granules, garlic, vinegar jalapeño juice and oregano. Boil for 5 minutes.

6. Add carrots and boil again for 10 minutes or until carrots are just tender.

7. Add chicken to pot as well as some of the oil that the chicken was cooked in.

8. In another pot bring 2 cups of water and the onion rings to a boil for 10 minutes, separating the onion rings.

INSTRUCTIONS (cont.):

9. When done, drain water and add onions to broth.

10. Simmer until ready to serve.

11. Divide into bowls and garnish with chopped cilantro and sliced lime sliced.

12. Serve with warm tortillas or a side of coconut rice.

TIPS:

- You can decrease the jalapeño juice to 1 Tbsp and add ½ fresh jalapeño chopped.
- If you're unable to find Mexican oregano, you can substitute regular (Mediterranean) oregano.

Chimole AKA Black Soup

Courtesy of Kimberly Wylie

INGREDIENTS:

½ cup Water

3 Tbsp Black Recado

1 tsp Ground Cumin

1 lb Ground Steak

1 Eggs, raw

½ tsp – Dried Mint

¾ tsp Salt

½ tsp Black Pepper

2 Tbsp Olive Oil

1 Whole Chicken, cut into pieces

4 cloves Garlic, minced

2 Fresh Oregano Leaves, chopped

4 Tomatoes, diced

1 Bell Pepper, diced

1 Onion, diced

6 Hard-Boiled Eggs, sliced – for garnish

Photo by Marie Sharp's

INSTRUCTIONS:

1. Preheat oven to 350° F.

2. In a small bowl, combine the black recado and cumin with the water. Set aside to dissolve.

3. In a separate bowl, mix the ground steak with the raw egg, mint, salt, and pepper.

4. Form into small, 1-inch diameter meatballs and bake on rimmed cookie sheet for 12 to 15 minutes.

5. While the meatballs are baking, heat the olive oil in a stock pot on medium-high heat.

6. Once hot, brown the chicken pieces with the garlic.

7. Once browned, fill the pot with water until the chicken is just covered and add the black recado and cumin liquid.

8. Add in the diced tomatoes, diced pepper, diced onion and oregano.

9. Bring to a boil, then turn heat down and simmer for 30 minutes.

10. Remove chicken from the soup, pull meat from the bones and add meat back to the pot.

11. Add the meat balls and simmer gently for another 5 minutes.

12. Ladle into bowls and garnish with slices of hard-boiled egg.

13. Serve with flour tortillas and coconut rice.

TIPS:

- If you like your soup thicker, in a separate bowl, mix 1 Tbsp cornstarch with 1/3 cup cold water and at slurry to soup at the end.
- Some folks don't bother pulling the meat from the chicken and serve the whole pieces with bones. If you'd like to do this, try using just legs and thighs to start, instead of a whole chicken.

Photo by L. Kelly Jones

Ms. Bella's Famous Stew(ed) Red Beans

Courtesy of Chef Bella of PUR Boutique Cabanas and Taco Bar

PURBoutiqueCabanas.com

Try these Ms. Bella's Famous Stew(ed) Red Beans, Stuffed Fry Jacks and more at PUR Boutique Cabana & Taco Bar! PUR is located on Ambergris Caye, just 1 mile north of the bridge. This is a wonderful stop for a social afternoon with a swim-up pool bar in one of the only adults-only settings on the island. Plus, they have the best (and the HUGEST) burritos on Ambergris

We recommend serving this with barbecued chicken, coleslaw, and a side like rice and beans or a large homemade tortilla.

INGREDIENTS:

2 lb Pinto or Red Beans

3 cloves Garlic, minced

1 small White Onion, diced

1 Green Pepper, diced

1 lb Bacon, chopped

1 (8 oz) can tomato sauce

1 bottle of Belikin beer

INSTRUCTIONS:

1. Wash beans thoroughly. Set in pan and add water until they are just covered, then add the garlic.

2. Place on fire (traditional) or stove top and simmer uncovered 1 1/2 hours, until beans are soft.

3. In a separate saucepan, stir-fry the onions, green peppers, and bacon.

4. When these are cooked, add to the beans, and add the tomato sauce and beer.

5. Add black pepper and salt to taste.

6. Let the mixture boil about 25 minutes to let flavors set; it is ready to serve at that point.

Rice and Beans (Belizian Style)

Courtesy of Nancy Lindley

INGREDIENTS:

1 cup Cooked Stewed Beans
   (see pg. 50)

½ lb Uncooked Rice

½ cup Coconut Milk

½ tsp Salt

$1/_8$ tsp Black Pepper

1 Tbsp Coconut Oil or
   Cooking Oil

1 Tbsp Green Pepper, diced

1 Tbsp Onion, diced

Photo by Olivera Rusu at Elvi's Kitchen

INSTRUCTIONS:

1. Add oil to pot and sauté green peppers and onions till translucent but not browned.

2. Wash rice and drain.

3. Add rice and sauté rice for 5 minutes stirring continuously.

4. Add stewed beans, coconut milk, salt and pepper.

5. Add water until it covers mixture and is ¾-inch above the rice.

6. Cook on high until mixture comes to a boil.

7. Reduce heat to low, cover and cook until rice is done; about 20 minutes.

Refried Beans

Courtesy of Nancy Lindley

INGREDIENTS:

1 lb Red Kidney Beans

1 Tbsp Salt

1 tsp Dried Oregano

4 cloves Garlic

3 Tbsp Cilantro, chopped

2 Bay Leaves

2 Tbsp Sweet Pepper, diced

½ cup Onion, diced

¼ cup Coconut Oil

5 cups Water

INSTRUCTIONS:

1. Wash beans and soak overnight in water.

2. Sauté onions, garlic and peppers in a small amount of coconut oil.

3. Bring beans to a boil and simmer for approximately 1 hour.

4. Blend beans and sautéed vegetables in blender until your preferred consistency.

5. Heat frying pan with coconut oil.

6. Add beans to frying pan and cook for about 10 minutes stirring constantly.

Vee's Cornbread

Courtesy of Cyndi McLean

INGREDIENTS:

4 Tbsp Butter

1 1/2 cups Cornmeal

1/2 cup Flour

1 tsp Baking Soda

1 tsp Salt

1 tsp Sugar

2 Eggs, beaten

1/4 cup Vegetable Oil

1 1/2 cups Buttermilk (substitute 1 1/2 cups Milk w/ 2 Tbsp Vinegar if necessary)

INSTRUCTIONS:

1. Preheat oven to 450° F.

2. Combine all dry ingredients in a bowl.

3. In a separate bowl, combine all wet ingredients, except butter.

4. Put butter in medium size cast iron skillet and place in oven. Allow butter to melt and skillet to get hot., swirling butter around edges of skillet to prevent sticking.

5. Pour remaining butter in wet ingredients.

6. Combine wet and dry ingredients using just enough strokes to combine ingredients.

7. Pour batter into warm iron skillet.

8. Bake 30-40 minutes until middle is done. Enjoy!

Coconut White Rice

Courtesy of Nancy Lindley

INGREDIENTS:

1 cup White Rice

1 ½ cups Water

½ cup Coconut Milk

¼ cup White Onion, diced

Coconut Oil

Pinch Salt

INSTRUCTIONS:

1. Rinse rice under running water for about 1 minute to wash the starch off the rice.

2. Heat pot on medium low heat, add coconut oil and then onions.

3. Sweat/simmer onion for 30 seconds.

4. Add rice into pot, cook for 20 seconds then add water, coconut milk, season with a pinch salt, and cover. The liquid should be approximately ¾" above the rice.

5. Turn heat to high and cook. Until the rice starts to show, approximately 10 to 12 minutes. Turn heat to low and cook for 4 minutes. Then turn off heat and leave to sit, covered, until rice is tender.

Cooking Chicken for San Pedro Hot Lunch

Belizean Cole Slaw

Courtesy of Kimberly Wylie

INGREDIENTS:

1 head Cabbage, medium

1 – Red Pepper

6 – Carrots

2/3 cup Mayonnaise

2 Tbsp Evaporated Milk

2 Tbsp Vinegar

3 Tbsp Sugar

1 Tbsp Olive Oil

Salt and Pepper (to taste)

INSTRUCTIONS:

1. **To make the dressing:** Whisk mayonnaise, evaporated milk, vinegar, sugar, olive oil, and salt and pepper in a large bowl until well-combined. Set aside and refrigerate.

2. Slice cabbage and red pepper very thin.

3. Grate carrots finely.

4. Combine veggies with dressing and toss to combine.

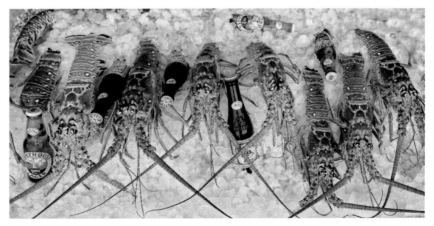

Photo by Olivera Rusu

BELIZEAN
MAIN DISHES

Belizean Stewed Chicken

Courtesy of Nancy Lindley

INGREDIENTS:

2 Bone-In Chicken Breasts

1 tsp Recado (see pg. 20)

½ tsp Salt

½ tsp Season All

1 tsp dried Oregano

2 pinches Black Pepper

4 cloves Garlic, minced

2 Tbsp White Sugar

2 Tbsp Coconut Oil

1 cup Water

1 cup Tomatoes, diced

1 cup Onion

INSTRUCTIONS:

1. Rub recado on chicken and then coat with remainder of seasonings – salt, Season All, oregano, pepper, and garlic.

3. Heat pan.

4. Add coconut oil and sugar to heated pan and brown the sugar.

5. Add chicken and cook for 2 minutes, turn and cook for another 2 minutes.

6. Add water, tomatoes and onion.

7. Cover and stew for 35 minutes or longer.

10. Mince chicken and serve.

Chicken Salbutes

Courtesy of Nancy Lindley

INGREDIENTS:

Belizean Stewed Chicken (see pg. 58)

Masa Dough (see pg. 22)

1 large Red Onion, diced

3 tsp Dried Oregano

¾ cup Orange Juice

1 Tbsp Salt

4 Tbsp Lime Juice

Oil of choice for frying

1 Tomato, diced

1 (4 oz.) can of Jalapenos, diced

INSTRUCTIONS:

1. Prepare onion curtido for topping, by combining onion, oregano, orange juice, salt and lime juice in a bowl. Set aside

2. Roll 1-inch masa dough ball into a circle approximately $1/8$-inch thick.

3. Heat oil in frying pan on medium heat. When hot fry each masa disc until golden brown. Drain well on paper towels.

4. Layer stewed chicken, then onion curtido, tomato and finally top with a jalapeno.

TIP:

- You can also top these with a little red cabbage and chopped cilantro to brighten them up.

Caliente's Coconut Chicken

Courtesy of Caliente Restaurant
Facebook.com/CalienteBelize/

Caliente is located right on the beach, in the heart of San Pedro, and is attached to the Spindrift Hotel. Since 2001, the team at Caliente has been serving a unique Caribbean-Mexican fusion cuisine. Sit out on the patio, enjoy a delicious lunch or dinner, and watch the people walking up and down the beach, while the tranquil, turquoise Caribbean sea laps gently at the shoreline. The owners of Caliente were kind enough to share one of my all-time favorite dishes for this cookbook – Coconut Chicken. Give it a try, when you come visit. I'm sure it'll become your favorite too!

INGREDIENTS:

6 to 8 cups Vegetable Oil

4 Chicken Breasts, boneless & skinless

½ cup Flour

2 cups Coconut, shredded

2 Eggs

Salt and Pepper to taste

INSTRUCTIONS:

1. Heat oil in medium size pot to 350° F.

2. Cut chicken breast into strips and season with salt and pepper.

3. Combine flour and coconut in a bowl.

4. In a separate bowl, beat the eggs.

5. One at a time, dip a chicken strip into the egg then into the coconut & flour mixture. Press the chicken into the coconut for full coverage.

6. Place strip into the oil and fry for 5 minutes, until golden brown.

7. Take out and pat dry with paper towels.

8. At Caliente, they serve this with a delicious orange citrus sauce!

Conchita Pibil (AKA Mayan Barbecue Pork)

Courtesy of Kimberly Wylie

Pibil is Belize's answer to pulled pork. "Pibil" means "buried" in Mayan and, as the name implies, originally the pork was cooked buried in a pit, covered in banana leaves.

You can use this yummy, tender pork on or in any number of things — tacos, enchiladas, tamales, or even pile it on top of a burger for an extra-special treat, like my friends at Losers do. Of course, my favorite way to eat it is all by itself, simply served with some coconut rice and a side salad.

INGREDIENTS:

3 lbs Boneless Pork Shoulder

½ cup Recado (see pg. 20)

2 cups Orange Juice

½ cup Lime Juice

3 cloves Garlic

3 tsp Kosher Salt

½ cup Lard or Unsalted Butter, melted

1 Red Onion, sliced

4 Bay Leaves

1 cup Water

INSTRUCTIONS:

1. Preheat oven to 350° F.

2. For marinade, place recado, juices, garlic, salt, and lard or butter in a blender and blend until smooth.

3. Line a large Dutch oven with banana leaves, place pork on banana leaves.

4. Pour marinade over pork, place onion slices and bay leaves over the top and wrap leaves around the roast. Secure with toothpicks, if you need to.

5. Add one cup water to the Dutch oven, put lid on and cook for 6 hours or until internal temperature reads at least 145° F.

6. Remove banana leaves and bay leaves, shred pork and mix with juices.

TIP:

- If you don't have a Dutch oven, you can use a deep baking dish and cover tightly with foil.

Belizean Chicken Tamales (AKA Bollos)

Courtesy of Kimberly Wylie

Makes 15 to 20 tamales

Belizean tamales are different from ones I was used to in the United States. When I first had them, I noticed the first difference was these are wrapped in banana leaves, not corn husks. Inside though was also significantly different, including the first ones I had were made with whole chicken wings – bones and all. My recipe uses boneless chicken breast instead. Just know if you enjoy one of these here on the island, it may or may not be made with bone-in chicken. Other differences include the preparation of the masa, as well as the inclusion of peas in the filling.

INGREDIENTS:

Stewed Chicken (see pg. 58)

1 White Onion, diced

½ bunch Cilantro Leaves, roughly
    chopped

8 oz Tomato Sauce

7 to 8 cups Water (divided)

3 lbs Masa Flour (divided)

1 tsp Lime Juice

2 tsp Salt (divided)

1 (15 oz) can Sweet Peas, drained

4 Tomatoes, diced

½ Jalapeno, minced (seeded and
    deveined if you don't like spicy)

Salt and Pepper to Taste

1 tsp Recado (see pg. 20) mixed with 2 Tbsp Water

2 Tbsp Lard or Unsalted Butter, melted

24 to 30 Banana Leaves

INSTRUCTIONS:

1. Prepare stewed chicken the night before, pull the meat from the bones and store in the refrigerator until ready to use.

2. **To make the "gravy"** – the middle part of the tamales: add 6 cups water, onions and cilantro to stock pot or Dutch oven, heat over medium heat and simmer for 15 minutes or until onions are soft.

3. Combine 2 ¼ pounds of masa with lime juice, 1 teaspoon salt and just enough water to make a paste, about the consistency of wallpaper paste.

4. Add tomato sauce to onions and cilantro then turn burner to low and pour masa paste through a strainer into the simmering tomato sauce/onion/cilantro pot. Stir as you strain into the pot, so it doesn't become lumpy. You may need to assist the masa through the strainer by stirring it in the strainer to push it through.

5. As the gravy becomes thicker continue to stir, add tomatoes, peas, jalapeno, recado slurry, and salt and pepper to taste. Your gravy should be a very thick, stew-like consistency.

6. **To make the outside of the tamales:** combine the remaining ¾ pound of masa flour and combine with just enough water to make a paste, then push through a strainer into a pot and add 1 tsp salt.

7. Over medium heat, stir in lard (or butter) and cook, stirring continuously, for 3 minutes, until fat is combined. You'll have a batter-like consistency, in the end.

8. Rinse your banana leaves. If they are not pliable, you can steam them a little.

9. Spread a very thin amount (think the amount you would use for a crepe) of the masa for the outside of the tamales, in a circle, on the center of the banana leaf. (I leave a couple of inches on each side free for folding.)

10. Add a generous scoop of gravy and a piece or two of the chicken.

11. To fold, bring the top and bottom edge of the banana leaf up to meat in the middle, directly over the filling. Fold these edges downward to the filling, then fold each end toward the center to close, kind of like the reverse way you would do a burrito, with the ends on the outside, and not on the inside.

12. Pull thin strips of extra banana leaf to make a tie. Tie pieces around to keep closed while cooking.

ALTERNATE: You can also make these without the banana leaves and use a piece of foil in place of the leaf. Fold in the same manner. No tying is needed, which makes it a little easier, but you do not get the subtle flavor from the banana leaf when cooking and they don't look as nice.

13. Place in a stock pot, cover with water and simmer gently for 1 hour, then remove and let cool at least one hour before unwrapping.

Lionfish Fingers with Garlic Dill Aioli

Courtesy of Maresha Reid of Pirate's Treasure & Pirate's Secret Beach
Facebook.com/PiratesTreasureRestaurantAndBar

Serves 2

Pirate's Treasure is located ½ mile north of the bridge. Pirate's Treasure combines a fun and lively bar, with yummy bar bites, with Maresha's Chef's Table – an amazing, personalized culinary experience, where Maresha whips up a multi-course meal, on an open hearth, right before your eyes!

Her second location – Pirate's Secret Beach – is the ultimate Secret Beach destination. Once you get to the Secret Beach area, just keep going straight and park. You'll find lots of loungers, with lots of shade. Tons of in-water tables are available for noshing on the best food in the Secret Beach area.

INGREDIENTS:

½ lb Lionfish Filet, cut into 6 to 8 fingers
    (can also use snapper, grouper, tilapia,
    or any white fish)

1 small Lime, juiced

1 Lime, cut into wedges

1 Egg (beaten)

2 cups All-Purpose Flour

4 cups Vegetable Oil

1 tsp Complete Seasoning

½ tsp Garlic Powder

½ tsp Ground Black Pepper

1 pinch Seasoned Salt

GARLIC DILL AIOLI INGREDIENTS:

½ cup Mayo

2 Tbsp Fresh Dill, finely chopped (or parsley or cilantro)

2 dashes Hot Sauce

1 tsp Fresh Garlic, chopped

1 drop Lime Juice

Salt and Pepper to taste

INSTRUCTIONS:

1. Prepare aioli first by mixing all aioli ingredients together then cover and refrigerate until serving time.

2. Place oil into an 8" deep frying pan on medium high heat (375° F).

3. Pour lime juice on fish fillet, sprinkle all spices evenly and rub gently to evenly spice each finger.

4. Individually coat each finger in flour then in egg wash. Individually and carefully in egg wash is key so as not to lose spices. Dip in flour once again, slightly compressing flour to adhere to egg wash.

5. Place a piece of paper towel onto a flat container to absorb excess oil after frying (near the cooking area).

6. Test oil by sprinkling a tiny pinch of flour into oil, it must immediately start sizzling and not just settle on top of oil.

7. Individually place each fish finger in oil once ready and gently stir in between each to avoid them sticking together. Do not flip right away. Allow to fry 3 to 4minutes until you see a golden ring around each one then flip. Once fully golden brown and crispy, remove with tongs, hover over pan for a few seconds to allow all oil to drip off then rest on paper towel for another minute.

8. Serve with lime wedges and garlic dill aioli. Enjoy!

The Chef's Table at Pirate's Treasure.

Curry Shrimp

Courtesy of Hidden Treasure

HiddenTreasureBelize.com

Serves 2

If you're looking for elegant, fine dining on Ambergris Caye - Hidden Treasure is where you need to be. This award-winning restaurant is tucked into the Escalante neighborhood, and truly is a hidden treasure! There is nothing more romantic than dining by candlelight, in rustic, but elegantly-appointed surroundings. Hidden Treasure is on my "must go" list when we have friends and family visiting.

INGREDIENTS:

2 Tbsp Cooking Oil

Fresh Garlic, finely chopped

28 medium Shrimp

1 Onion, julienned

1 Bell Pepper, julienned

1 tsp Curry Powder

½ tsp Salt

Pinch Black Pepper

1 cup Coconut Milk

Red Pepper Flakes (optional)

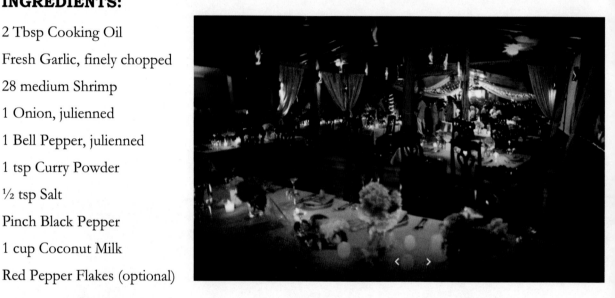

INSTRUCTIONS:

1. Heat oil in large frying pan on medium heat, add garlic and cook for 10 seconds.

2. Add shrimp, onion, bell pepper, curry powder, salt, black pepper, and red pepper flakes, if using.

3. Let cook for 60 seconds then add coconut milk. Bring to a boil and cook for an additional 30 seconds.

4. Divide among two plates, with a side of rice, and serve.

Fish Panades

Courtesy of Kieron Lennan

Often referred to as a Belizean meat pie, a panades is similar to an empanada. It can be sweet or savory, but is most often filled with either fish or beans. It is usually served with a cabbage, onion and pepper salsa topping..

This particular recipe is from the kitchen of Kieron Lennan, a Red Seal Chef and Friend who lives in San Pedro, Belize.

INGREDIENTS:

Masa Dough (see pg. 22)

½ cabbage or onion

Vinegar

1 tsp Cilantro, chopped

1 medium White Onion, diced

½ Sweet Pepper (red, green, yellow, or orange), diced

3 cloves Garlic, minced

½ tsp Lime Juice

½ lb Fish

1 tsp Black Pepper

Salt to taste

INSTRUCTIONS:

1. Prepare the slaw by chopping cabbage finely and soak in vinegar and a generous amount of salt for at least an hour.

2. Drain vinegar and rinse with water, then add onion, sweet pepper, garlic and lime juice to bowl. Salt to taste and set aside.

3. Add all seasonings to fish.

4. On a grill or in a pan, cook on high heat for 5 minutes, flip it and leave for another 5 minutes then mince fish.

5. Roll 1-inch masa balls into a circle ⅛-inch thick.

6. Add minced fish to the center of the circle and fold, pressing edges to seal closed.

7. Heat oil on medium heat until hot and fry until golden brown.

8. Drain on paper towels.

9. Plate and garnish with cabbage/onion sauce on top.

10. Eat/Enjoy

Caribbean Grouper with Mango Salsa on Mashers

Courtesy of Lolly Slattery

Serves 4

INGREDIENTS:

4 large Potatoes

¼ cup Media Crema

2 Tbsp Butter

4 Fresh Skinless Grouper Filets

Banana Leaves

4 Limes (divided)

Salt and Pepper to taste

3 Ripe Mangoes

1 Seedless Jalapeno, diced

1 small bunch Cilantro, chopped

2 Roma Tomatoes, diced

1 clove Garlic, minced

INSTRUCTIONS:

1. Preheat oven to 350° F.

2. Peel and cube potatoes and boil until soft.

3. Strain, add cream and butter, whip and keep warm.

4. Fold grouper into banana leaves with juice of 1 lime and salt and pepper, to make a square packet.

5. Turn seam side down in glass casserole dish and bake for 15 to 20 minutes.

6. While fish bakes, dice mango, tomatoes, cilantro, garlic and seeded jalapeno in bowl and squeeze two limes on liberally.

7. Combine and add salt and pepper to taste.

8. For plating, put mashers on center of plate with filet on top. Smother with salsa, garnish with lime slices.

Fish Sere

Courtesy of Kimberly Wylie

INGREDIENTS:

1 Grouper, cleaned and fileted

2 Tbsp Cooking Oil

2 Tbsp Pork Fat

3 Plantains, green

A splash Coconut Cream

3 cups Coconut Milk

Salt to taste

1 White Onion, diced

1 Carrot, diced

1 Jalapeno, minced

2 White Potatoes, diced

Cilantro, chopped for garnish

INSTRUCTIONS:

1. Heat oil in frying pan and sear both sides of the fish filets. Remove from pan and set aside.

2. Add pork fat and onions to pan and cook until translucent and slightly caramelized. Remove from pan and set aside.

3. Grate plantains and add just enough coconut cream to form a dough. Add salt to taste and form into small dumplings.

4. In a stock pot, bring coconut milk and water to a boil. Add onion, carrot, jalapeno, and potatoes to the pot, along with the dumplings. Simmer for 20 minutes or until potatoes are tender.

5. In the last 5 minutes, add the fish to the pot so it is just submerged in the broth.

6. Serve with coconut rice or mashed potatoes and garnished with cilantro.

BELIZEAN DESSERTS

Ginger Snap Key Lime Pie

Courtesy of Lolly Slattery

Serves 6 to 8

INGREDIENTS:

1 1/2 cups Gingersnap
   Cookies, crumbled

3 Tbsp Brown Sugar

1/2 tsp Ground Ginger

6 Tbsp Butter, melted

3 cups Sweetened Condensed
   Milk

½ cup Sour Cream

¾ cup Key Lime Juice

1 Tbsp Lime Zest, grated

INSTRUCTIONS:

1. Preheat oven to 350° F.

2. Combine cookies, brown sugar, ginger and butter and press into greased 9-inch pie pan.

3. Bake for 10 minutes and then let completely cool.

4. Mix sweetened condensed milk, sour cream, lime juice, and lime zest together until smooth.

5. Pour into cooled pie crust.

6. Bake for 8 minutes.

7. Chill completely before serving.

8. Garnish with lime slices and enjoy!

Cyndi Lou's Pineapple Upside Down Banana Bread

Courtesy of Cyndi McLean

INGREDIENTS:

3 Tbsp Butter

½ cup Raw Brown Sugar - divided

1 cup Pineapple, diced

2 cups Flour

1 tsp Baking Powder

1 tsp Baking Soda

1 tsp Salt

3 to 4 Ripe Bananas, mashed

¼ cup Vegetable Oil

2 Eggs, beaten

INSTRUCTIONS:

1. Preheat oven to 325° F.

2. Place medium iron skillet with butter in oven.

3. When butter is melted, swirl around edges of skillet to prevent sticking.

4. Sprinkle ¼ cup raw brown sugar in remaining butter.

5. Scatter pineapple on top of butter mixture.

6. In a bowl, mix all dry ingredients together, including the remaining ¼ cup of raw brown sugar.

7. In a separate bowl, mix bananas, oil and eggs.

8. Combine wet and dry ingredients using a few strokes, just enough to combine ingredients, and pour on top of pineapple mixture.

9. Bake 30 to 35 minutes. Check middle to make sure it is done.

10. Remove from oven and immediately turn skillet upside down onto clean surface of your choice. Your Pineapple Upside Down Banana Bread should fall right out.

Paletas

Courtesy of Nancy Lindley

INGREDIENTS:

3 cups Ripe Fruit (fresh or frozen)

½ cup Sugar

$\frac{1}{3}$ cup Water

3 Tbsp Lime or Lemon Juice

Paper Cups & Wooden Sticks

INSTRUCTIONS:

1. Place half of the fruit, sugar, water, and lime juice into a blender and blend until smooth.

2. Dice the other half of the fruit.

3. Spoon diced fruit into cups, then add the blended mixture, leaving about ½-inch of headspace for expansion.

4. Place cups into freezer and allow at least six hours to firm the treat up.

5. Take pops out of the freezer for about an hour, insert wooden sticks into the slushy mix, then return to freezer.

©Olivera Rusu

Photo by Olivera Rusu

VARIATIONS:

- Blend all the fruit.
- Vary the liquid – instead of water you can try fruit juice, vegetable juice, tea, milk, or cream.
- Pick your sweetener. Instead of sugar, use agave nectar, honey, syrup, or artificial sweeteners
- Add something "hot." It is not uncommon to add a touch of powdered chili to cut fruit in Belize.
- Add something "cool." Fresh mint leaves, or mint syrup, or a small amount of spearmint, or peppermint essence can be added.

Sweet Potato Pone

Courtesy of Nancy Lindley

INGREDIENTS:

1 lb Sweet Potato, grated (white flesh if available)

1 cup Evaporated Milk

1 cup Coconut Milk

1 tsp Vanilla

½ tsp Nutmeg

½ tsp Cinnamon

¼ cup Ginger, grated

⅛ cup Coconut Rum

INSTRUCTIONS:

1. Preheat oven to 350° F.

2. Mix all ingredients together.

3. Very lightly grease a 12-cup muffin tray.

4. Fill muffin tins.

5. Bake for about 80 minutes. The pones should caramelize on the outside and set like pumpkin pie.

6. Serve warm

Photo by Olivera Rusu

Lime Pie

Courtesy of Nancy Lindley

INGREDIENTS:

2 cups All-Purpose Flour

½ tsp Salt

5 Tbsp Vegetable Shortening or Butter

6 to 7 Tbsp Cold Water, as needed

1 (14 oz.) can Sweetened Condensed Milk

6 Eggs, separated

8 tsp White Sugar

¼ tsp Cream of Tartar

$\frac{1}{3}$ cup Lime Juice

1 tsp Lime Zest

INSTRUCTIONS:

1. Preheat oven to 400° F.

2. Mix together flour and salt.

3. Cut in shortening or butter until coarse crumbs form.

4. Add water, a little at a time, and mix until a ball forms. Add more water or use less to get the dough to a rolling consistency.

5. Roll dough on a floured surface to around a 10" circle or about the size of your baking dish. Place dough in pan, prick with a fork and bake for 15 minutes or until its golden brown. Take out and leave to cool.

6. Reduce heat in oven to 325° F.

7. Beat egg yolks in a bowl.

8. Fold in condensed milk, lime juice, lime zest and cream of tartar.

INSTRUCTIONS (cont.):

9. In a separate bowl, beat egg whites until they reach soft peaks.

10. Add sugar to egg whites gradually and beat until eggs reach stiff peaks.

11. Add condensed milk mixture to crust and bake for 25 minutes.

11. Turn oven up to 425° F.

12. Top pie with egg whites.

13. Return to oven and bake 5 to 7 minutes until meringue is golden brown.

14. When finished baking take out oven and leave to cool to help it set and become more firm.

15. TIME TO ENJOY!

Photo by Olivera Rusu

BELIZEAN DRINKS

Lolly's Frozen Coconut Mojito

Courtesy of Lolly Slattery

Serves 4 (Unless it's Kim and Lolly, then only serves 2)

INGREDIENTS:

½ full Blender with Ice

5 oz. Coco Lopez

Handful of Mint Leaves (no stems)

6 Limes, squeezed with pulp

2 shots White Rum

2 shots Dark Rum

INSTRUCTIONS:

1. Add all ingredients to blender.

2. Blend until smooth.

3. Garnish with lime slice and a sprig of mint!

Panty Ripper AKA Pantiripa

Courtesy of Kimberly Wylie

Serves 1

You'll find Panty Rippers served all over the island. All feature three ingredients – coconut rum, pineapple juice and grenadine. I'll admit, I like mine strong and sweet. Feel free to adjust the ingredients to your taste – and alcohol tolerance.

INGREDIENTS:

2 oz Coconut Rum

2 oz Pineapple Juice

1 count (approx.. 1 Tbsp) Grenadine Syrup

Ice

INSTRUCTIONS:

1. Pour all ingredients into a drink shaker and shake.

2. Pour all ingredients into a glass, sit by the ocean and enjoy!

Photo courtesy of Rebecca Coutant
author, *Fifty Big Experiences on Ambergris Caye, Belize*
SanPedroScoop.com

Rum Punch

Courtesy of Kimberly Wylie

Serves…well, depends on your friends. Makes 1 quart.

If you go out on a boat tour, chances are you're going to be treated to some complimentary rum punch – obviously after all water activities have been completed. We want to keep you safe! Cold rum punch is so refreshing after a day in the Caribbean sun.

INGREDIENTS:

2 ½ cups Orange Juice

2 ½ cups Pineapple Juice

¼ cup Coconut Rum

¼ cup Banana Rum

1 cup White Rum

1 cup Dark Rum

2 Limes, juiced

¼ cup Grenadine Syrup

Ice

INSTRUCTIONS:

1. Mix all ingredients, except ice, in a 2-quart pitcher.

2. Top with ice, until you have about 1 ½ quarts volume, and stir again.

3. Serve and enjoy with friends and start planning your next trip to Ambergris Caye!

Photo by Olivera Rusu at Las Terrazas

Watermelon Daiquiri

Courtesy of Kimberly Wylie

Makes 1 Quart

Watermelon is plentiful in Belize and so deliciously sweet and juicy! Combine readily-available watermelon and readily-available rum, and watermelon daiquiris are a natural result.

INGREDIENTS:

6 cups Watermelon Fruit, diced and seeds removed

½ cup White Rum

¼ cup Coconut Rum

¼ cup Orange Juice

2 Limes, juiced

Ice

INSTRUCTIONS:

1. Place watermelon and liquid ingredients into blender.

2. Add ice to bring blender 8 cup-level.

3. Blend until smooth.

TIP:

- If your watermelon isn't sweet enough, or you just like your drinks extra-sweet (like me), then add a couple of tablespoons of honey.

Making food for San Pedro Hot Lunch Program

PADDLEBOARDS

Photo by L. Kelly Jones

NON-BELIZEAN Cuisine

BREAKFASTS

Holiday French Toast

Courtesy of Aleta Hidinger

INGREDIENTS:

2 Tbsp Butter

4 Eggs

½ cup Orange Juice

½ cup Cream

1 (8 oz.) can Crushed Pineapple

¼ cup Sugar

1 Tbsp Orange Zest, grated

½ tsp Vanilla

¼ tsp Nutmeg

1 loaf French Bread (cut into 1-inch slices)

½ cup Pecans, chopped

¼ cup Butter (softened)

½ cup Brown Sugar, firmly packed

1 Tbsp Light Corn Syrup

½ cup Pecans, chopped (optional)

INSTRUCTIONS:

1. The night before, melt 2 tablespoons butter in a 9x13 inch pan and place bread in pan.

2. Combine eggs, orange juice, cream, pineapple, sugar, zest, vanilla, nutmeg, and half-cup pecans in a bowl.

3. Pour over bread.

4. Combine ¼ cup butter, brown sugar and corn syrup.

5. Spread this topping over the bread then sprinkle with nuts (if desired).

6. Cover and refrigerate overnight.

7. The next morning, preheat oven to 350° F.

8. Bake 40 minutes or until golden brown.

Grandma Dorothy's Caramel Rolls

Courtesy of Jenna Lambert

INGREDIENTS:

1 package Dry Yeast

½ cup Warm Water (105° to 115° F)

½ cup Warm Milk, scalded and cooled

$2/3$ cup Sugar

$1/3$ cup Butter

1 tsp Salt

3 ½ to 4 cups Flour

1 Egg

3 ½ to 4 cups Flour

1 ¼ cups Brown Sugar, packed

1 ½ sticks Butter

2 Tbsp Milk or Half and Half

2 Tbsp Ground Cinnamon

INSTRUCTIONS:

1. Dissolve yeast in warm water. Stir in scalded milk, $2/3$ cup sugar, egg, $1/3$ cup butter, salt and 2 cups of flour.

2. Beat until smooth.

3. Stir in enough remaining flour to make dough easy to handle.

4. Turn onto a floured surface and knead approximately 5 minutes, until smooth and elastic.

5. Place in a greased bowl and let rise until double, approximately 90 minutes.

6. In a metal 9 x 12 baking dish, melt butter, sugar and milk over low heat, stirring constantly until sugar is dissolved.

7. Remove from heat and set aside.

9. Preheat oven to 350° F.

10. When dough is risen, punch down dough and roll out into a rectangle, ¼-thick.

11. Sprinkle dough with cinnamon.

12. Cut dough into 12 equal strips, tie each strip into a knot and place in cake pan on top of caramel.

13. Cover pan with clean dish towel and let rise until double, approximately 1 hour.

14. Bake for 30 to 35 minutes, until golden brown.

15. Remove from oven and immediately turn upside down on to a cookie sheet.

Breakfast Pockets

Courtesy of Kimberly Wylie

INGREDIENTS:

1 ½ Tbsp Yeast

½ cup Warm Water (110 degrees)

¾ cup Evaporated Milk, warmed (110 degrees)

½ cup Butter, melted

¼ cup Brown Sugar

1 Egg

1 tsp Salt

3 to 4 cups All-Purpose Flour

1 (32 oz.) bag Frozen Hash Browns

6 Eggs

1 Tbsp Butter

½ lb Cheddar Cheese, shredded

1lb Breakfast Sausage, ground

Salt and Pepper to taste

Photo by Olivera Rusu at Athens Gate

INSTRUCTIONS:

1. Preheat oven to 350° F.

2. Combine yeast, water, evaporated milk, brown sugar, melted butter, egg, and salt in large bowl.

3. Add flour ½ cup at a time, until you have a soft but not overly sticky dough.

4. Knead for 5 minutes.

5. Cover bowl with a clean dish towel and place in a warm spot to rise for 30 minutes.

6. While your dough is rising, prepare your filling ingredients.

7. Add butter and eggs to cold frying pan and scramble over medium heat, stirring constantly. Place in bowl and set aside.

8. Cook hash browns per package instructions. Place in bowl and set aside.

9. Brown breakfast sausage, breaking into crumbles.

INSTRUCTIONS (cont.):

10. Combine eggs, hash browns, sausage and shredded cheese.

11. Divide dough into 12 pieces, roll out into a circle until very thin – approximately $\frac{1}{16}$-inch thick.

12. Fill and fold like a burrito.

13. Place seam side down on a cookie sheet and bake for 12 to 15 minutes until golden brown.

TIP:

- These freeze beautifully! Make a double batch and cool after cooking. Then place on a cookie sheet to freeze individually. Once frozen, place in freezer storage bags. To reheat, place in microwave for 60 to 90 seconds until heated through.

Photo by Grant Wylie

Better Than Cinnabon Cinnamon Rolls

Courtesy of Kimberly Wylie

For me, there's one primary reason to go to the mall – Cinnabon Cinnamon Rolls. Those ooey-gooey, majestic rolls of decadence are just absolutely delicious. Needless to say, when we moved to Ambergris Caye we said goodbye to malls and Cinnabon, so I developed this recipe to take care of my cinnamon craving. It's a time consuming, recipe but oh-so-worth it!

This dough can be made by hand; however, a stand mixer will make your life so much easier.

INGREDIENTS:

2 ¼ tsp Active Dry Yeast

1 cup Warm Water (105°F)

½ cup Sugar

7 Tbsp Unsalted Butter, divided

¼ cup Milk

1 Tbsp + 1 tsp Lemon Juice

2 large Eggs

5 ½ to 6 cups All-Purpose Flour

1 ½ tsp Salt

1 cup Salted Butter, softened (divided)

1 ½ cups Dark Brown Sugar

2 Tbsp Ground Cinnamon

1 tsp Cornstarch

8 oz Cream Cheese, softened

1 Tbsp Vanilla

¼ tsp Salt

2 cups Powdered Sugar

INSTRUCTIONS:

1. Pour water and sugar into the bowl of a stand mixer and sprinkle yeast over top.

2. Melt 6 tablespoons of unsalted butter in a microwave safe bowl.

3. In a separate bowl, combine milk and lemon juice.

4. Add butter, milk mixture, egg and salt to yeast mixture in the stand mixer's bowl.

5. Fit mixer with dough hook and beginning kneading, adding flour ½ cup at a time.

6. Continue to add flour until the dough comes cleanly from the sides and the dough is no longer overly sticky. Dough should be tacky, but not sticky.

7. Continue to need for 5 minutes.

8. Remove dough from bowl and coat the bowl with the remaining 1 tablespoon of melted unsalted butter.

INSTRUCTIONS (cont.):

9. Place dough back in mixing bowl, swirl around to coat the dough lightly in butter, flip upside down, then cover the bowl with a clean dishcloth.

10. Place dough in oven with oven light on and allow to rise for 60 minutes. (Leaving just the oven light on will keep the interior of your oven just warm enough to proof your dough.

11. Combine brown sugar, cinnamon and corn starch in separate bowl and set aside.

12. Turn dough out onto lightly floured surface.

13. Knock air out and roll out into an 18" by 24" rectangle.

14. Spread ½ cup of salted butter on dough.

15. Sprinkle buttered dough with brown sugar mixture.

16. Use rolling pin to gently press sugar into butter, to prevent it from falling out as you roll the dough.

17. Grease two 9" x 13" baking dishes.

18. Roll the dough toward you tightly, starting from the longest end.

19. Cut the dough into twelve 2-inch slices.

20. Place six rolls in each pan, evenly spacing them.

21. Loosely cover each baking dish with plastic wrap, to keep the rolls moist, and place back in the oven with JUST the oven light on to proof another 60 minutes.

22. Remove baking dishes from oven and preheat oven to 350° F.

23. Bake for 18 to 22 minutes, until rolls are golden brown and cooked through.

24. While rolls are baking, add cream cheese, remaining ½ cup butter, lemon juice, vanilla, and salt into a clean mixing bowl.

25. Beat until light and fluffy.

26. Slowly add powdered sugar and continue to beat until fluffy.

27. When rolls are cooked through, remove from oven and spread ¼ of the frosting on the rolls.

28. Allow rolls to cool slightly and spread remaining frosting.

29. Serve and enjoy!

From Scratch Biscuits & Gravy

Courtesy of Kimberly Wylie

Once you make these biscuits, you'll never buy those preservative-filled can poppers again!

INGREDIENTS:

1 cup Milk, cold

1 tsp Lemon Juice

2 cups Flour

4 tsp Baking Powder

¼ tsp Baking Soda

¾ tsp Salt

4 Tbsp Salted Butter

1 lb Breakfast Sausage, ground

2 Tbsp Salted Butter

¼ cup Flour

2 cups Milk

Salt and Pepper to taste

INSTRUCTIONS:

1. Preheat oven to 450° F.

2. Mix lemon juice into milk and set aside.

3. In a large mixing bowl, combine flour, baking powder, baking soda and salt.

4. Cut butter into dry ingredients, with either a pastry cutter, a fork, two knives, or your fingertips. Work quickly, as you don't want the butter to melt.

5. Make a well in the center and pour in the chilled milk mixture.

6. Stir just enough until the dough comes together. The dough will be VERY sticky.

7. Turn dough onto floured surface, dust the top with flour and gently fold dough over on itself 5 times, adding flour if it's still very sticky. Do NOT overwork the dough.

8. Press dough into a 1-inch thick round.

9. Cut out biscuits with a 2-inch cutter, being sure to push straight down through the dough and flour the cutter between each cut.

INSTRUCTIONS (cont.):

10. Place biscuits on baking sheet so they just touch.

11. Reform scrap dough, working it as little as possible and continue cutting. (Biscuits from the second pass will not be quite as light as those from the first, but hey, that's life.)

12. Bake until biscuits are tall and light golden brown on top, 15 to 20 minutes.

13. While the biscuits bake, brown and crumble the sausage in a skillet. Do not drain.

14. Add butter to the skillet.

15. Once melted, add flour and mix. The flour will basically coat the sausage and almost disappear.

16. Slowly add milk, stirring constantly then heat over medium-high heat until bubbly and thick.

17. Add salt and pepper to taste.

18. To serve, slice warm biscuits open and top with decadent gravy and tuck in!

TIPS:

- I like to line my baking sheet with parchment paper to save on clean up. Non-stick aluminum foil works as well.
- If you don't have a biscuit cutter, you can use a glass that's approximately 2-inch in diameter.
- Don't be afraid to go a little heavy on the pepper in the gravy.

Photo by L. Kelly Jones

Grandma's Pancakes

Courtesy of Alexandria Boiton Williams of
Paco's Secret Beach, Paco's Tiki Bar and Paco's Pot Pies
Facebook.com/PacosPotPies/

Serves 6

Miss Alexandria is a single mother of twin boys who has been cooking for as long as she can remember. As co-owner of Paco's Secret Beach and Paco's Tiki Bar (best coconut mojito you can buy on the island!), the COVID19 pandemic hit her and her children hard. After many sleepless nights, she came up with Paco's Pot Pies. Using a recipe that has been wowing family and friends for years, she realized it was the perfect food to set up for delivery, during the quarantine. These 10" loaded pot pies have quickly become a favorite! Once the island reopens, you'll be able to purchase them through special order for the upcoming Paco's Pot Pies Facebook page, or enjoy them on the beach at either Paco's Secret Beach or Paco's Tiki Bar.

"We can choose to see stress as a challenge, not a setback." I chose to challenge myself.
~Alexandria Boiton Williams

INGREDIENTS:

1 ½ cups All Purpose Flour

3 tsp Baking Powder

½ tsp Salt

1 Tbsp White Sugar

1 cup Milk

1 tsp Vanilla

1 Egg

2 Tbsp Butter, melted

Photo by Olivera Rusu

INSTRUCTIONS:

1. In a mixing bowl, combine flour, baking powder, salt, and sugar.

2. Add egg, milk and melted butter and mix until smooth.

3. Butter griddle and heat on medium.

4. Pour ¼ cup batter per pancake on griddle and cook until golden brown with a slight crisp.

5. Flip and repeat on other side, then serve and enjoy

Strawberries & Cream Crepes

Courtesy of Kimberly Wylie

INGREDIENTS:

1 cup Whipping Cream

3 Tbsp Sugar (divided)

2 Eggs

1 ¼ cup Milk

1 cup Flour

1 tsp Vanilla

2 Tbsp Butter

1 pint Strawberries, sliced

Powdered sugar for garnish

INSTRUCTIONS:

1. **To make whipped cream:** Place whipping cream and 2 tablespoons of sugar in a cold metal bowl and whip to stiff peaks.

2. Set aside and refrigerate.

3. **To make crepes:** Place eggs, milk, flour, vanilla, and 1 tablespoon of sugar in a blender. Blend for 10 seconds, until just mixed.

4. Place crepe mixture in refrigerator for at least 30 minutes.

5. Heat a small frying pan and add a little butter to the pan.

6. Pour a small amount of batter into the pan and tilt the pan to evenly coat the bottom with a thin layer.

7. Allow to cook for 30 seconds then flip and cook the other side.

8. Once all crepes are cooked, combine strawberries with the whipped cream.

9. Place a small amount of strawberries and cream onto one end of the crepe and roll up to serve.

10. Sprinkle with powdered sugar.

APPETIZERS

Cod Skin with Cured Egg Yolk

Courtesy of Chef Robin Halling - Private Chef, Restaurant Consultant, Head Chef
ChefRobinHalling.wixsite.com/mysite

Robin Halling is a gourmet chef who has worked in several Michelin star restaurants. Whether he's whipping up culinary masterpieces for visitors to Ambergris Caye, on a private yacht or in a luxury chalet, Robin's cuisine focuses on sustainable, locally-sourced ingredients that will delight your palate.

INGREDIENTS:

Cod Skin from 1 Fish

10 Egg Yolks

Soy Sauce

1kg Watercress

1 Mackerel

2 Tbsp Dijon Mustard

4 Tbsp Apple Cider Vinegar

350g Vegetable Oil

Salt and pepper

Dill

INSTRUCTIONS:

1. Cure 8 egg yolks in salt and soy sauce for 4 days then push the egg yolks through a sieve and save.

2. Scrape the cod skin so there's no meat left on the skin, dry it out either in the oven or a dehydrator, until completely dry, and cut into 2×2 cm squares then deep fry in hot oil. It will pop, so be careful. Leave to rest on the side.

3. Filet your mackerel, pull off the skin season with salt, pepper and chopped dill on the filet and let rest for 4 hours.

4. Wash of the salt and dry the fish.

5. Dehydrate 800g of watercress until completely dry and grind to a powder.

6. Put 2 egg yolks in a bowl with the mustard and start whipping, slowly adding the oil to make a mayonnaise

7. Add 200g of finely chopped watercress to mayonnaise and season with apple cider vinegar and salt.

ASSEMBLE:

1. On top of the cod skin, pipe the cold egg yolk cream, also pipe the cold mayonnaise.

2. Cut the mackerel into cubes and put on top.

3. Dust with watercress powder and garnish with edible flowers or some fresh foraged wild herbs.

House Roasted Jalapeno & Chorizo Queso

Courtesy of Rum Dog Bar & Grill

Facebook.com/RumDogBZ/

Located just 1 mile north of the bridge, Rum Dog offers the most amazing over-the-water drinks and food on the island. This isn't your ordinary bar grub. Rum Dog offers elevated (both literally and metaphorically) pub cuisine, with a Belizean flair. Friendly service and awe-inspiring views of the reef, Rum Dog is one of my personal favorite spots to eat.

INGREDIENTS:

6 large Jalapeños

1 Tbsp Olive Oil

½ lb Sausage or Chorizo

¾ cup Onion, diced

¾ cup Tomato, diced

1 lb Velveeta Cheese, cubed

Tortilla Chips

INSTRUCTIONS:

1. Preheat oven to 475° F.

2. Halve and seed 5 of the jalapeños, toss with oil in a bowl, and put on a baking sheet – skin side up.

3. Roast until very dark, about 20 minutes. Keep an eye out though.

4. Let cool and then chop very fine.

5. Mince the raw jalapeño with seeds and all.

6. Cook sausage and onion in a saucepan until meat is cooked and onion is translucent, about 8 minutes.

7. Stir in tomatoes and roasted jalapeños.

8. Add the cheese one cube at a time until melted and smooth.

9. Add the raw jalapeño and stir.

10. Serve with tortilla chips.

Basil, Sun-Dried Tomato & Feta Cheese Foldovers

Courtesy of Kimberly Wylie

INGREDIENTS:

1 Egg Yolk

1 tsp Water

8 oz. Feta Cheese

1 Egg

1 Tbsp Green Onion, thinly-sliced

3 Fresh Basil Leaves – thinly sliced

1 Sun Dried Tomato - minced

1 (17.5 ounce) box Frozen Puff Pastry

INSTRUCTIONS:

1. Preheat oven to 375 F.

2. In a small bowl, beat egg yolk with 1 teaspoon water and set aside.

3. In a separate bowl, crumble cheese and blend with the whole egg, green onions, sun dried tomatoes and basil.

4. Cut thawed pastry into twelve 3 inch squares.

5. Place a mounded tablespoon of filling in the center of each square.

6. Moisten edges with water and fold pastry over filling to form a triangle and press edges together firmly with a fork to seal.

7. Brush tops lightly with egg yolk mixture and bake for 20 minutes or until golden brown.

9. Serve warm or at room temperature.

Photo by Olivera Rusu

TIPS:

- You can also take this filling and bake into phyllo cups.
- To slice the basil leaves, roll each leaf lengthwise into a tight tube, then thinly slice from one end.
- You can also add thinly sliced spinach, if you'd like, instead of basil and sun-dried tomato.
- These can be made the night before and kept in the fridge until you're ready to bake. Perfect for pre-party planning!

Cheese Crackers

Courtesy Kimberly Wylie

INGREDIENTS:

10 oz Extra Sharp Cheddar cheese, from block not pre-shredded

1 ½ cups All-Purpose Flour

½ cup Salted Butter, cut into pieces and slightly softened

1 tsp Salt

½ tsp Dried Oregano

½ tsp Ground Cayenne Pepper

2 Tbsp Heavy Cream

INSTRUCTIONS:

1. Preheat oven to 350° F.

2. Dice cheese into 1-inch cubes.

Photo by Grant Wylie

3. Pulse cheese, flour, butter, salt, oregano, and cayenne pepper in food processor until mixture resembles crumbs.

4. Add cream and process for 8 to 12 seconds, until the dough forms a ball.

5. Turn out dough onto floured surface and cut in half.

6. Roll each half into a $1/8$-inch thickness.

7. Cut out cracker shapes with cookie cutters that are between 2 ½ and 3 ½ inches. Stars, flowers, butterflies, etc. are all popular. Or look at holiday shaped cutters, such as pumpkins or bunnies.

8. Place cut outs on parchment-lined baking sheet. Ensure crackers are 2 inches apart.

9. Bake 16 to 18 minutes then cool on baking sheets placed on wire racks for at least 30 minutes.

TIPS:

- Dough can be made ahead of time and wrapped in plastic wrap, then placed in a zip top bag, up to three days in advance.
- Be sure to position your cut outs as close together as possible, ensuring as little dough is left over as possible, as the dough will get tough if it's re rolled.
- Do not use pre-shredded cheddar for this recipe, as shredded cheese is often coated by the manufacturer to keep it from sticking together in the bag

Photo by Olivera Rusu
at Las Terrazas

SOUPS, SALADS & SIDE DISHES

Island Buddha Bowls

Courtesy of Lolly Slattery

Serves 4

INGREDIENTS:

1 cup Dried Couscous

1 (15 oz.) can Corn

1 (16 oz.) can Garbanzo Beans

3 Carrots, shredded

2 Avocados, sliced

¼ head Purple Cabbage, shredded

¼ head White Cabbage, shredded

1 Jicama, shredded

Olive Oil

Salt and Pepper

INSTRUCTIONS:

1. Prepare couscous as directed on package.

2. Spoon cooked couscous into bottom of bowl.

3. Layer remaining ingredients on top of couscous.

4. Drizzle with olive oil and salt and pepper to taste.

Kim's Chicken Tortilla Soup

Kimberly Wylie

Serves 6

INGREDIENTS:

2 Tbsp Olive Oil

½ Red Onion, diced

3 cloves Garlic, minced

1 Jalapeno, seeded and diced

2 tsp Salt

2 Tbsp Chili Powder

3 Tbsp Tomato Paste

12 cups Chicken Broth

6 Beef Bouillon Cubes

½ lb Cooked Chicken, pulled into pieces

1 handful Cilantro Leaves, roughly chopped

4 Tbsp Lime Juice

Tortilla chips

Photo by Olivera Rusu

INGREDIENTS:

1. In stock pot over medium, sauté onion, garlic and jalapeno in olive oil until all are soft and translucent.

2. Add salt, chili powder and tomato paste and mix thoroughly.

3. Slowly add chicken broth, beef cubes and chicken. Stir to combine.

4. Simmer, stirring occasionally for 20 minutes.

5. Just before serving, toss in cilantro leaves and lime juice.

6. Serve in bowls sprinkle with crushed tortilla chips.

TIP:

- Other yummy toppings include: shredded sharp cheddar cheese, crumbled cotija cheese and/or a dollop of sour cream.

Belikin Stout Chili

Courtesy of Kimberly Wylie

Serves 12

INGREDIENTS:

2 Tbsp Ground Cumin

10 Tbsp Chili Powder

1 tsp Ground Coriander

½ tsp Cayenne Powder

5 lb Ground Beef. Lean

2 Tbsp Olive Oil

2 ½ lb Vidalia Onions, diced

Sour Cream

Extra-Sharp Cheddar Cheese, shredded

1 ½ lb Red Bell Peppers, diced

1 ½ lb Yellow Bell Peppers, diced

5 cloves Garlic, minced

2 (28 oz.) cans Crushed Tomatoes, undrained

2 (15 oz.) cans Kidney Beans, drained

1 bottle Belikin Stout

1 to 2 large Jalapeños, finely diced

Chopped Green Onions

INSTRUCTIONS:

1. Sauté beef in heavy large stock pot over medium-high heat.

2. Heat oil in large skillet over medium-high heat. Add onions, all bell peppers, and jalapeños. Sauté until vegetables begin to soften, about 15 minutes.

3. Add mixture to pot with meat. Mix in spices and crushed tomatoes, beans, and beer.

4. Bring chili to boil, stirring occasionally. Reduce heat and simmer 20 minutes, stirring often.

5. Season with salt and pepper, ladle chili into bowls. Serve with sour cream, green onions, and cheese.

TIPS:

If you like a thicker chili try one of these methods for thickening, once your chili comes to a simmer.

- Sprinkle a little masa or corn meal over the top of your simmering chili. Mix in and allow to thicken.
- Tear up a corn or flour tortilla into very small pieces and stir into simmering chili. Allow to cook, stirring occasionally, until dissolved and chili is thickened.
- Add 2 Tbsp corn starch to a small amount of cold water and mix thoroughly. Stir slurry into simmering chili to thicken.

Belikin Stout French Onion Soup

Courtesy of Kimberly Wylie

Serves 6

3 lb Vidalia or Walla Walla Onions, sliced

2 cloves Garlic - minced

¼ cup Unsalted Butter

2 Tbsp Olive Oil

½ tsp Black Pepper

½ tsp Sugar

6 cups Beef Broth

4 bottles Belikin Stout Beer

3 Tbsp Flour

2 tsp Beef Bouillon

Baguette slices, toasted

2 cups White Cheddar, shredded

1 cup Swiss Cheese, shredded

INSTRUCTIONS:

1. In a large pot, melt butter over medium-high heat. Add onion, reduce heat to low, cover and cook for 15 minutes.

2. Turn heat up to medium, add salt, pepper, sugar, and garlic powder and continue to cook for 40 minutes, stirring occasionally.

3. Add flour to onions and stir. Slowly stir in broth and then beer.

4. Simmer uncovered for one hour. Season with salt and pepper to taste.

5. Preheat oven to 350° F.

6. Combine cheddar and Swiss cheese in a bowl.

7. Divide the soup into oven-safe bowls and top with toast and a cheeses.

8. Turn oven to broil and broil until the cheese is golden brown.

Grilled Corn with Lime Butter

Courtesy of Kimberly Wylie

INGREDIENTS:

1 ½ Tbsp Butter, melted

¼ tsp Lime Rind, grated

2 Tbsp Lime Juice

¼ tsp Salt

¼ tsp Ground Cayenne Pepper

8 ears Corn, unshucked

8 oz Cotija, Chihuahua or Feta Cheese

INSTRUCTIONS:

1. Soak corn WITH husks on, in cold water for 30 minutes

2. Preheat your grill.

3. Combine butter, rind, juice, salt and pepper in a small bowl and set aside.

4. Place corn directly on grill rack

5. Cook 10 minutes, turning frequently. Do not worry if corn husks burn.

6. Remove from heat and allow to cool just enough to handle safely.

7. Cut ends off corn cobs, then squeeze corn out of husks. (Notice how there are almost none of those annoying cornsilk strands? You're welcome!)

8. Brush corn with butter mixture and sprinkle on cheese.

Lots of volunteers make the San Pedro Hot Lunch Program a reality.

Warm Potato Salad

Courtesy of Nancy Lindley

INGREDIENTS:

4 to 5 lb Potatoes, cubed (baby potatoes are nice, a mix of sweet potatoes, white and red is also nice)

1 to 2 cups Frozen Corn

1 Onion

3 to 5 cloves Garlic, finely diced

1 (16 oz.) package Bacon

½ cup Parmesan Cheese

1 ½ cups Asiago Cheese, grated

1 ½ cups Sour Cream

1 ½ cups Mayo

Olive Oil

Dill to taste

Salt and Pepper to taste

Photo by Grant Wylie

INSTRUCTIONS:

1. Fry up bacon and crumble (save some of the bacon grease)

2. Boil potatoes (leave them a bit underdone)

3. Cut into bite size pieces.

4. Sprinkle a bit of olive oil and bacon fat over potatoes, toss. All the potatoes should be lightly coated.

5. Spread potatoes on baking sheets.

6. Sprinkle corn, minced garlic, dill, a touch of salt and pepper over mixture.

7. Roast at 425°F until crispy (you will need to turn them).

8. Mix together sour cream, mayo, parmesan cheese, asiago cheese.

9. Toss roasted potatoes, bacon, and dressing - serve warm. Can also be placed into a casserole dish and baked at 350°F for 20-30 minutes until everything is nice and bubbly.

Photo by Olivera Rusu
at Cayo Espanto

MAIN COURSES

Truffle Pecorino Cream with Grilled Onion and Apple

Courtesy of Chef Robin Halling - Private Chef, Restaurant Consultant, Head Chef
ChefRobinHalling.wixsite.com/mysite

Serves 2

Robin Halling began his career in the Michelin Restaurant Lindsay House by Richard Corrigan. He worked his way up to become the food enthusiast he is. Robin then moved on to Bagatelle, a two-star Michelin restaurant in Norway, where he started as a Chef de Partie and then quickly moved on to Sous Chef and was part of achieving the second Michelin star. With two gold medals and one silver in the Swedish BBQ Association, he creates culinary delights in everything from barbeque to luxury caterings to fine dining. Sustainable produce and foraging is a high priority, for Robin. Perfection, creativity and hard work are the words that describe him. As an integral part of several Michelin kitchens around the world, and as a private chef at yacht and chalets, he is used to high-end, fast-paced that exceed the expectations of his guests.

CREAM SAUCE INGREDIENTS:

500g Pecorino

½ Black Truffle

200g Cream

Salt and Pepper (to taste)

20g Olive Oil

Yellow or White Onions

CREAM SAUCE INSTRUCTIONS:

1. Grate pecorino and truffle in a food processor.

2. Boil cream and add to the food processor.

3. Add olive oil and blend until a fine puree. Add salt and pepper to taste.

4. Keep in a warm place or on top of a water bath to keep the consistency of a fondue.

5. Cut yellow or white onions in half and grill them on one side, you want them to be black but not overcooked.

6. Separate the onions and bake in oven on 400° F (200° C) for approximately 7 to 10 minutes. It's important to keep the nice texture of the onions.

CHICKEN STOCK SAUCE INGREDIENTS:

10 Chicken Wings

1 liter Water

500g Apple Juice

1 Lemon

200g Tapioca

1 Onion

1/2 Garlic Bulb

Thyme

1 Carrot

2 stems Celery

1 Tbsp Butter

CHICKEN STOCK SAUCE INSTRUCTIONS:

1. Roast chicken wings until golden.

2. Put the butter in a pot over medium heat and add thinly sliced vegetables and thyme.

3. Add chicken wings, cover with water and simmer for 3 hours.

4. Add apple juice and simmer for another hour then strain the stock and continue to cook until reduced by half.

6. Add the tapioca and let simmer until tapioca is softened.

7. Add salt and pepper to taste and, at the end, grated lemon zest and juice to freshen up the sauce.

THYME OIL INGREDIENTS:

50g Spinach

150g Olive Oil

50g Thyme

THYME OIL INSTRUCTIONS:

1. Warm the oil with spinach and thyme.

2. Add to blender and blend for 3 minutes then strain

ASSEMBLY:

1. Put the cheese mix on the bottom of the plate add your onions on top.

2. Reheat your chicken and tapioca sauce and split it with the thyme oil.

3. Top cheese mixture with sauce at a ratio of 80/20 and garnish with fresh thyme. Nasturtium also works very good as a garnish with thyme leaves.

Crock Pot Chicken Chili

Courtesy of Stella's Sunset Wine Bar
Facebook.com/StellasWine/

Serves 6 to 8

Stella's Sunset is one of my personal favorite places to have dinner. Set on the western coast of Ambergris Caye, 1 mile north of the bridge, the sunsets are AMAZING at Stella's! Sit on the water's edge, enjoy a nice glass of wine from their extensive list, savor a delicious meal, and watch the sun slowly dipping below the horizon, turn the sky a kaleidoscope of colors from orange to purple. Several nights a week, you can even sit under the stars and listen to live music.

A note from Stella's Sunset:

The beauty of this is you can use what you have on hand. Have fun and get creative!

INGREDIENTS:

2 Chicken Breast, boneless & skinless or 2 cups of Rotisserie Chicken, cooked & cubed

1 (16 oz) can or 2 cups Black Beans, drained & rinsed

1 (16 oz) can of other Beans (Red, Pinto, etc.). drained & rinsed

2 (14 ½ oz) cans Diced Tomatoes, drained or 5 to 6 Fresh Tomatoes, diced

1 (15 ¼ oz) can corn, drained & rinsed

½ cup Onion, diced

2 cups Chicken Broth

1 Bell Pepper, diced

1 Jalapeño, minced (remove seeds & ribs)

1 tsp Salt

1 Tbsp Ground Cumin

2 tsp Chili Powder

2 tsp Dried Oregano

4 oz Cream Cheese (optional)

INSTRUCTIONS:

1. Add all ingredients, except cream cheese, to your crock-pot.

2. Cook on low 6 to 7 hours or on high for 3 hours.

3. Remove chicken breasts and shred or chop into bite size pieces, return to crock-pot.

4. If making creamy version add cream cheese.

5. Taste season with salt, pepper, chili etc. and cover and cook another 15 minutes or so while you gather chili fixins' like fresh chopped cilantro, shredded cheese, sour cream, lime wedge.

6. Serve with tortilla chips, rice etc.

STOVE TOP INSTRUCTIONS:

1. Chop chicken and lightly brown in 1 Tbsp oil in soup pot.

2. Add onions and other veggies and cook until onions are softened.

3. Then dump in the rest of the ingredients (except if adding cream cheese) and simmer on low heat 40 to 45 minutes until chicken is cooked through and tender.

4. Add cream cheese 5 minutes before serving and continue like above.

Stella's Sunset Wine Bar

BBQ Chicken Pizza with Pineapple Jalapeno Salsa

Courtesy of Shannon Reeder of Iguana Juan's
IguanaJuans2018.wixsite.com/IguanaJuans

I remember the first time I heard about Iguana Juan's. A girl was wearing a shirt that said they were "conveniently located upstairs of an old building, on a Back Street, on an island in Central America." I said – "I need to go there!" And go there I did. From fajitas to prime rib to tamales to Fourth of July specials including apple pie, there is always something yummy at this cool restaurant. Sit out on the patio tables, listen to live music and enjoy some people watching along Back Street.

SALSA INGREDIENTS:

1 Pineapple, cut into small cubes

1 large White Onion, chopped

4 Jalapenos, diced

BARBECUE SAUCE INGREDIENTS:

5 cups Ketchup (divided)

2 cups Siracha (divided)

3 Tbsp Yellow Mustard

4 Tbsp Worcestershire Sauce

2 Tbsp Brown Sugar

1 Tbsp Garlic Powder

1 Tbsp Onion Powder

2 tsp Black Pepper

1 tsp Chili Powder

1 tsp Paprika

2 tsp Complete Seasoning (or sub 1 tsp Salt)

1 cup Water

TORTILLA INGREDIENTS:

1 lb Flour

1 tsp Salt

1 Tbsp Baking Soda

½ cup Water

1 tsp Crisco

CHICKEN INGREDIENTS:

1 lb Chicken Breast, boneless & skinless (trimmed of fat)

Red Recado mixed with a little water (see pg. 20) or substitute Paprika, Garlic, Salt and/or Chili Powder to taste.

Shredded Mozzarella

Cilantro, roughly chopped

INSTRUCTIONS:

1. For salsa, combine pineapple, jalapenos, and onions in a bowl and set aside.

2. For barbeque sauce, in a large pot combine 4 cups ketchup, 1 cup siracha, mustard, worchestershire sauce, brown sugar, garlic powder, onion powder, pepper, chili powder, paprika, and Complete Seasoning. Cook over medium heat, until bubbles begin to pop, then add one cup of water.

3. Stir well and heat for a few more minutes, then turn off heat and let cool on the stove.

4. Once cool, mix with remaining 1 cup ketchup and 1 cup siracha (or less if you don't want that extra kick!). NOTE: This yields a little more than a half-gallon of sauce. It keeps well in the fridge, and you can use for all your BBQ Sauce needs!

5. For tortillas, mix flour, salt, baking soda, water, and Crisco together well and let stand for approximately 40 to 45 minutes, covered with container or plastic wrap.

6. Roll into small balls, then take a large piece of foil and cover with Crisco or other vegetable oil. Put one ball on the foil, pat out into a large, round tortilla and place on a hot comal or flat cast iron skillet.

7. Leave tortilla in a pan over medium heat for 30 seconds covered with foil. Remove foil, flip, and cook other side until desired color.

8. Preheat oven to 350° F.

9. For the chicken, season chicken with recado or spices of your choice and bake for 25 minutes.

10. Cool and shred.

11. Preheat your grill.

12. To assemble your pizza, place a tortilla on the grill and cover with BBQ sauce. Top with shredded chicken, shredded mozzarella and pineapple jalapeno salsa.

13. Remove once the cheese has melted, and top with chopped cilantro. Enjoy!

Asparagus Stuffed Chicken Breast

Courtesy of Kimberly Wylie

Serves 4

INGREDIENTS:

4 Chicken Breasts, boneless & skinless

½ tsp Dried Oregano

½ tsp Dried Basil

1 tsp Garlic Powder

1 tsp Smoked Paprika

Salt and pepper to taste

1 medium Tomato, diced

4 oz Mozzarella Cheese, shredded

12 Asparagus Stalks, ends trimmed

1 Tbsp Olive Oil

Optional: Balsamic Glaze

INSTRUCTIONS:

1. Preheat oven to 350° F.

2. In a small mixing bowl, mix together oregano, basil, garlic powder, paprika, salt, and pepper and set aside.

3. Place the chicken breast between two sheets of waxed paper or cling wrap and pound to ¼-inch thickness and sprinkle each breast with the seasoning mixture then top with mozzarella and tomatoes.

4. At one end of each breast, add 3 sprigs of asparagus and roll up chicken breast from this end around the asparagus spears.

5. Fasten chicken breasts closed with toothpicks

6. Heat oil in skillet and sear each chicken breast until nicely golden brown, about 3 to 5 minutes per side.

7. Transfer chicken to baking dish and cover with foil and bake for 15 to 20 minutes or until chicken reaches an internal temperature of 165° F.

TIP:

- After plating, drizzle a little balsamic glaze over the top of each breast, for an extra special treat!

Photo by Olivera Rusu at Azul Resort

Super Easy Chicken & Dumplings

Courtesy of Kimberly Wylie

Serves 8

INGREDIENTS:

1 Roasted Chicken (or a couple of pounds of leftover chicken from another meal)

1 (49 oz.) can Chicken Broth

6 cups Chicken Bouillon

1 (26 oz.) can Cream of Chicken Soup

½ bag of sliced frozen mix vegetables

½ Tbsp Poultry Seasoning

8 Tbsp Corn Starch

½ cup Cold Water

2 cups Flour

4 tsp Baking Powder

1 tsp Salt

¼ tsp Pepper

1 Egg, beaten

2 Tbsp Butter, melted

¾ to 1 cup Milk

*Chickens cooking for the
San Pedro Hot Lunch Program*

INSTRUCTIONS:

1. Make dumpling dough by mixing together flour, baking powder, salt, pepper, egg, butter, and just enough milk to make a relatively sticky dough. Set aside.

2. Bring chicken, broth, bouillon, soup, vegetables, and poultry season to a boil.

3. In a small bowl, mix corn starch and cold water.

4. Slowly add corn starch slurry to boiling chicken and broth, stirring as it's added. Allow to boil for 2 minutes.

5. Add dumplings by tablespoonfuls (larger if you like more biscuit-y dumplings) to the boiling liquid.

6. Cover and simmer for 18 minutes.

Crazy Canucks' Chicken Fajitas

Courtesy of Crazy Canucks
Facebook.com/CrazyCanucksBeachBar/

Crazy Canucks Beach Bar sets the standard for beach bars on Ambergris Caye. Your toes in the sand and cold drinks in your hand, I really can't think of a better way to spend my day. Rob and Krista always make sure there's something fun going on. Live music, charity bingo, and you really can't say you've been to the island if you haven't gone and watched the hermit crab races.

INGREDIENTS:

¼ cup Olive Oil

1/3 cup Fresh Lime Juice

1 tsp White Sugar

1 ¼ tsp Salt

¼ tsp Cumin

2 cloves Garlic, minced

¼ cup Water

Cheese, Sour Cream, Salsa, Lettuce, Cilantro, etc

1 ½ tsp Paprika

1 tsp Onion Powder

1 ½ Tbsp Chili Powder

2 lb Chicken Breasts, boneless & skinless

2 Onions, thinly sliced (yellow or white)

3 Bell Peppers, thinly sliced (any color)

Tortilas

INSTRUCTIONS:

1. Wisk together oil, lime juice, sugar, salt, cumin, garlic, water, paprika, onion powder, chili powder until thoroughly combined.

2. Place chicken, onions and peppers in Ziploc bag and add the above mixture.

3. Marinade in refrigerator for at least one hour (overnight is recommended).

4. Heat olive oil in large pan over medium heat.

5. Add chicken and pepper mixture (I add 1 to 2 servings at a time) and cook for 6 to 8 minutes, stirring occasionally, until chicken is cooked through and vegetables are tender.

6. Serve over rice or tortilla with your favorite toppings.

Orange Balsamic Chicken Breasts

Courtesy of Kimberly Wylie

Serves 8

INGREDIENTS:

½ cup Chicken Broth

½ cup Balsamic Vinegar

¼ cup Green Onion, finely diced

¼ cup Brown Sugar, packed

¼ tsp Orange Rind, grated

¼ cup Fresh Orange Juice

¾ tsp Salt (divided)

16 Chicken Thighs, boneless & skinless

Cooking Spray

½ tsp Freshly Ground Black Pepper

Orange Rind Strips (optional)

INSTRUCTIONS:

1. Preheat oven to 450° F.

*Spaghetti for the
San Pedro Hot Lunch Program*

2. Combine chicken broth, balsamic vinegar, green onion, brown sugar, orange rind, orange juice, and orange zest in a small saucepan and bring to a boil.

2. Reduce heat and simmer until reduced to 1/2 cup (about 20 minutes).

3. Stir in ¼ teaspoon salt.

4. Arrange chicken in a single layer in the bottom of a roasting pan coated with cooking spray and sprinkle chicken evenly with remaining ½ teaspoon salt and pepper.

5. Bake for 10 minutes.

6. Brush half of broth mixture over chicken. Bake 5 minutes. Brush remaining broth mixture over chicken and bake 15 minutes or until a thermometer registers 165° F.

7. Garnish with orange rind, if desired.

Kim's Tamales

Courtesy of Kimberly Wylie

Before we moved to Belize, I didn't know there were different types of tamales. These are the Mexican-style tamales, like you'll find in the States. They are delicious, but they are time consuming. This is a great project for you and a loved one to help with. Make a double batch and freeze them.

INGREDIENTS:

60 corn husks

2 lb Chicken Breast, boneless & skinless

1/2 Yellow Onion

2 cloves Garlic, minced

2 tsp Poultry Seasoning

1 tsp Salt

Black Pepper - to taste

7 cups Water

1 (10 oz) can red enchilada sauce

1 (10 oz) can green enchilada sauce

3/4 cup Lard

6 cups Masa Harina

1 Tbsp Salt

1 ½ tsp Baking Powder

1 Tbsp Sugar

6 cups Reserved Broth from chicken

INSTRUCTIONS:

1. Place corn husks in warm water. Weigh them down with a plate or bowl, and let them soak for at least 20 minutes.

2. Boil chicken, onion, garlic, poultry seasoning, salt and pepper in 7 cups of water, until chicken is cooked through.

3. Remove the chicken from the broth and save the broth and shred chicken.

4. Divide the chicken in half and place in two separate bowls. Add the red sauce to one pot. Add the green sauce to the other.

5. Mix the lard with your mixer on medium speed for a couple of minutes, until fluffy.

6. Mix salt, baking powder and sugar into cornmeal.

7. Turn mixer to lowest setting and slowly add 1 cup cornmeal mixture and then 1 c. broth.

8. Make sure it's completely mixed and then continue adding cornmeal and broth. In the end, the masa will be kind of damp PlayDoh-y in texture.

9. Open up a corn husk, place a small amount of masa on the husk - you want a square about half the width of the husk's width and almost 2/3 the height.

10. Smoosh it with your fingers into a rectangle shape, so the bottom of the square is about 1/3 up from the pointy end of the husk and centered width wise. Leaving about a ¼ to ½-inch of space at the top of the husk. Don't use too much masa - the rectangle should be no more than 1/4" thick.

11. Place a small amount of filling from one of the bowls in the center. Make a line down the center of the masa square, about 1/3 in width of the masa.

12. Bring the sides of the corn husks together, so the masa covers the filling (some may not be completely covered - that's OK! - then wrap the husks together one way around the tamale.

13. Fold the end of the husk up, around the bottom of the tamale.

14. Tear one of the extra husks into small ¼-inch strips and tie around the bottom of the wrapped tamale, so the folded end is tied in place. Tie a 2nd corn husk strip around the top to further secure the husk around the tamale.

15. If you have a steamer pot, place your insert in the bottom and fill with water until just below the insert and place all tamales in the pot, standing on end, folded end down - open end up.

16. Cover the pot, turn on high until the water starts to boil. Turn down to simmer and steam for 40 minutes, then cool, unwrap and enjoy!

TIPS:

- If you don't have access to lard, you can use unsalted butter in its place.
- If you don't have a steamer pot. I have taken a metal colander and a stock pot, where it fit so the handles of the colander kept it hanging in the top of the pot. And used that as a steamer. However, I had to cook them in batches that way – as all the tamales wouldn't fit.
- Make the chicken the night before, so it's one less step you have to do on tamale day.
- On Ambergris Caye, I sometimes have trouble finding enchilada sauce. When that happens, I substitute two 7 oz cans of Salsa Casera for the red enchilada sauce and/or two 7 oz cans of Salsa Verde for the green enchilada sauce. It's equally tasty!
- To differentiate between the red and green tamales take a dot of red or green food coloring and put it on the appropriate tamales.

Chicken at the Ritz

Dave Kendall

INGREDIENTS:

Cooking Spray

5 to 6 Chicken Breasts, boneless & skinless, pre-cooked & cut up

2 (10 ½ oz) can Cream of Chicken Soup

1 cup Sour Cream

½ cup Butter

1 sleeve Ritz Crackers, crushed

INSTRUCTIONS:

1. Preheat oven to 350° F.

2. Spray a 9x13 casserole dish with cooking spray.

3. Layer pre-cooked chicken breast pieces in bottom of casserole dish.

4. Mix Cream of Chicken soup with sour cream and spread over chicken.

5. Melt one stick of butter and combine with crushed Ritz crackers

6. Spread over soup layer and bake for 30 minutes.

Okie Apricot Chicken

Courtesy of Julie Kendall

INGREDIENTS:

8 Chicken Breasts, boneless & skinless

1 Tbsp Butter

1 Tbsp Vegetable Oil

1 cup Apricot Jam

1 cup Catalina Salad Dressing

2 to 3 Tbsp Onion Soup Mix

INSTRUCTIONS:

1. In large skillet, brown chicken in butter and oil over medium heat for 3 minutes on each side or until lightly browned.

2. Combine the apricot jam, salad dressing and soup mix; pour over the chicken.

3. Cover and simmer for 10 minutes or until juices run clear.

Photo by Olivera Rusu at Cayo Espanto

North Beach Retreat Beef Stew and Mashed Potatoes

Courtesy of Kristin Alvey of North Beach Retreat

NorthBeachRetreat.com

Serves 4

Located 9 miles north, North Beach Retreat is the cutest bed and breakfast on the beach you'll find on the island. You'll find the quiet tranquility you can only get at the north end of the island. If you'd like to wake up to the sound of birds and the reef crashing just offshore, you need to visit North Beach. To top it all off, the NBR staff whip up freshly-cooked breakfasts for their guests every morning and can arrange dinners for you as well. This hearty beef stew is just one of the many culinary delights you can experience during your stay.

INGREDIENTS:

2 lb Beef, ½" to 1" cubed

1 large Yellow Onion, sliced

8 cloves Garlic, minced

1 to 2 Habanero Peppers

1 cup Cilantro, roughly chopped (divided)

2 Tbsp Olive Oil

$1/3$ cup Balsamic Vinegar

¼ cup Soy Sauce

3 oz Tomato Paste

1 pinch Thyme

1 cup Water

Salt and Pepper to taste

½ head Cabbage, quartered

2 medium Carrots, 1-inch pieces

2 lb Potatoes, White or Russet

4 Tbsp Butter

1 cup Milk

INSTRUCTIONS:

1. Add 1 tablespoon olive oil to heated soup pot or Instant Pot and brown beef, seasoning generously with black pepper and a pinch of salt, over medium heat. Remove from pot and set aside, including juices.

2. In same pot, add 1 tablespoon olive oil and slice onions and sauté for 2 minutes.

3. Add tomato paste, oregano and thyme and continue to sauté for 3 more minutes.

4. Add garlic and sauté 1 more minute.

5. Deglaze the pot by pouring 1 cup water into pot and scrubbing the bottom with a wooden spoon to get the tasty stuff that has stuck to the pot off and into the broth.

6. Add balsamic vinegar, soy sauce, half of the cilantro, and beef into the pot. Make sure beef is at least partially submerged in the liquid.

7. Add carrots to the top of the pot and mix in.

8. If using Instant Pot – cook for 20 minutes under pressure then allow to depressurize for 20 minutes. Add cabbage and cook until soft.

9. If cooking on the stovetop – bring stew to a simmer, cover and cook for approximately 2 hours. Add cabbage with approximately 20 minutes remaining.

10. To finish off the stew, you can smash some of the carrots to thicken the broth, being careful with the beef as it will be very tender. You can also pull out some of the broth and cool with an ice cube or two, and add flour or corn starch to make a thickening slurry. Add back to the pot and allow to thicken.

11. Toward the end of the cooking time for the stew, place cubed potatoes into a large pot of water, with an added pinch of salt, and boil for 15 minutes.

12. Once soft, pour off water and add butter and half ot he milk in the pot and smash. (I use an old fashioned hand masher, as I like some firmer chunks, but a hand mixer works well, if you like them really smooth.)

13. Add additional milk to get desired consistency, and add salt and pepper to taste. (I try and balance this with how savory the stew tastes at this point.)

14. We serve this dish in a couple ways. Ff you like your stew thick, place onto a plate with a generous portion of potatoes. When it is more soupy we serve the stew in a bowl and the potatoes on a large plate.

15. Garnish with remaining cilantro and serve.

Kim's Awesome Italian Meatballs

Courtesy of Kimberly Wylie

I first made this recipe for a spaghetti dinner fundraiser my church hosted to raise money for holiday food baskets for those in need. I needed an easy recipe, that would allow me to make hundreds of meatballs. Everyone raved about them! What they didn't know - the secret ingredient to these meatballs is the mint. I know it may sound weird, but it works!

INGREDIENTS:

4 oz Butter, melted

2 tsp Garlic, minced

½ cup Italian-Seasoned Breadcrumbs

1 lb Ground Beef

1 tsp Dried Mint

1 egg

INSTRUCTIONS:

1. Preheat oven to 350° F.

2. Mix all ingredients by hand, until everything is just mixed.

3. Gently form into 8 balls and place on greased roasting pan rack.

4. Bake for 25 minutes.

TIP:

- Do NOT overwork your meatball mixture. Mixing it too much or handling them too much when you're forming the balls can make them tough.
- These are awesome with spaghetti sauce or in meatball subs, calzones or on pizza!

Better than IKEA Swedish Meatballs

Courtesy of Kimberly Wylie

Serves 6

I love wandering through IKEA. I also admit I love their Swedish meatballs. Living in Belize has meant no IKEAs and, therefore, no cheap and easy places to enjoy Swedish meatballs. So I developed this recipe that I honestly think is better. I hope you do too!

INGREDIENTS:

2 lb Ground Beef (90% lean)

2 Eggs

½ cup Bread Crumbs

1 tsp Salt

½ tsp Black Pepper

1 tsp Garlic Powder

1 clove Garlic, minced

3 Tbsp Butter

1 ½ cups Beef Bouillon (divided)

¼ cup Flour

1 ½ cups Sour Cream

1/8 tsp Nutmeg

1 lb Egg Noodles

Fresh parsley for garnish

Lingonberry Jam

INSTRUCTIONS:

1. Preheat oven to 350° F.

2. Mix ground beef, eggs, bread crumbs, salt, pepper, and garlic powder gently together.

3. Form into 32 meatballs and bake for 30 minutes or until done.

4. Meanwhile, sauté minced garlic in butter then add 1 cup beef bouillon and heat to boiling.

5. Whisk in flour into ½ cup reserved bullion. Once bouillon is boiling, slowly add in flour mixture.

6. Boil 1 minute and then stir in sour cream, season with nutmeg and heat through.

7. Combine sauce with meatballs.

8. In a separate pot, prepare egg noodles per instructions on package.

9. Serve meatballs over egg noodles alongside a side of lingonberry sauce.

TIP:

- If you can't find lingonberry sauce, whole cranberry sauce is a good accompaniment.

Lomo Saltado

Courtesy of Kimberly Wylie

Serves 4

This Peruvian dish is one of my family favorites. In fact, when my son comes to visit, it's always the dish he asks me to make. It's best to have all ingredients measured out and prepared, as it comes together quite quickly.

INGREDIENTS:

1 ½ to 2 lb Sirloin Steak, cut 1x2 inches pieces

1 Red Onion, diced

1 (28 oz) bag Frozen Steak Fries

1 Banana Pepper, diced

1 (26 oz) can Diced Tomatoes

2 Tbsp Fresh Parsley, chopped

½ Tbsp Balsamic Vinegar

4 cups White Rice, prepared with garlic and salt

$1/8$ cup White Vinegar

1 Tbsp Teriyaki Sauce

Olive Oil as needed

2 Tbsp Lime Juice

Salt and Pepper to taste

INSTRUCTIONS:

1. In wok, on medium-high heat, fry steak fries in approx. 2 Tbsp olive oil and salt to taste. Set aside on plate.

2. In the wok, fry the sirloin until just-cooked (when the juices begin to release) with salt and pepper and 2 Tbsp olive oil. Remove and place on plate next to fries.

3. If needed, add more oil and sauté the onions for about two minutes and then add the tomatoes.

4. Add salt, pepper, parsley and yellow pepper. Cook until tomato is a bit soft.

Photo by Olivera Rusu

5. Put the meat back in the wok and add the balsamic vinegar, white vinegar, soy sauce and lime . Mix well and heat on high until heated through.

6. Plate with a cup of rice one side of the plate; on the other side, put the fries with the meat mixture on top of the fries.

Soft Taco Bake

Courtesy of Nancy Lindley

INGREDIENTS:

4 (8-inch) Soft Taco Shells

2 cups Ground Beef

1 (10 ½ oz) can Tomato Soup

2 to 3 cups Grated Cheese

Taco Seasoning to taste

Optional Ingredients:

Onion

Hot Sauce

Green Peppers

Mushrooms

INSTRUCTIONS:

1. Preheat oven to 350° F.

2. Brown ground beef in a skillet on medium-low heat until there is absolutely no pink.

3. If you are adding onions add now and continue to cook until onions are slightly transparent.

4. Add tomato soup and a little bit of water (I usually put in about ½ of the soup can of water and use the water to rinse out the remaining soup in the can).

5. Season with taco seasoning (to your taste buds) – you could also add green peppers and mushrooms.

6. Simmer the mixture for 5 to 10 minutes so the seasonings are absorbed by the meat and tomato soup.

7. Add about 1 ½ cups of your cheese and stir until cheese is blended in and take off the heat.

8. In an 8-inch spring form pan or cake pan, put a soft taco shell on bottom, add a thin layer of meat mixture.

9. Add another shell, and then more meat mixture.

10. Continue building layers until you run out of meat mixture, ending with a shell on top.

11. Sprinkle the remaining cheese on the top of the last soft taco shell.

12. Bake for 15 minutes or until the cheese is melted and starting to brown.

13. Serve with salsa and sour cream.

Big pots are needed for the hundreds of free meals served at San Pedro Hot Lunch

Carne Asada Tacos

Courtesy of Kimberly Wylie

INGREDIENTS:

2 lb Flank or Skirt Steak, trimmed of excess fat

Olive Oil, for coating the grill

Kosher Salt and Freshly Ground Black Pepper

For Mojo:

6 Garlic Cloves, minced

1 Jalapeno, minced

1 handful Cilantro Leaves, finely chopped

1 tsp Salt

1 tsp Pepper

2 Limes, juiced

1 Orange, juiced

2 Tbsp White Vinegar

½ cup Olive Oil

For Salsa:

4 Plum Tomatoes, diced

½ medium Red Onion, diced

2 Green Onions, white and green parts, sliced

1 handful Cilantro Leaves, chopped

1 (4 oz) can Green Chiles, diced

1 lime, juiced

Salt to taste

Optional – Jalapeno, diced – amount to taste

For Assembly:

16 (7-inch) Corn Tortillas

White Onion, chopped for serving

8 oz Cotija Cheese

2 Limes, cut in wedges for serving

INSTRUCTIONS:

1. Combine all salsa ingredient in a bowl and refrigerate.

2. In a food processor, blend together the garlic, jalapeno, cilantro, salt, and pepper to make a paste.

3. Put the paste in a glass jar or plastic container with a lid. Add the lime juice, orange juice, vinegar, and oil. Shake it up really well to combine.

4. Lay the flank steak in a large baking dish and pour the mojo over it. Wrap tightly in plastic wrap and refrigerate for 1 hour or up to 8 hours, so the flavors can sink into the meat. Don't marinate the steak for more than 8 hours though, or the fibers break down too much and the meat gets mushy.

5. Preheat an outdoor grill or a ridged grill pan over medium-high flame (you can also use a broiler). Brush the grates with a little oil to prevent the meat from sticking.

6. Pull the steak out of the mojo marinade and season the steak on both sides with salt and pepper.

7. Grill (or broil) the steak for 7 to 10 minutes per side, turning once, until medium-rare.

8. Remove the steak to a cutting board and let it rest for 5 minutes to allow the juices to settle. Thinly slice the steak across the grain on a diagonal.

9. Warm the tortillas for 30 seconds on each side in a dry skillet or on the grill, until toasty and pliable.

10. **To make the tacos:** stack up 2 of the warm tortillas, lay about 4 ounces of beef down the center, and sprinkle with onion, cilantro and cheese. Top each taco with a spoonful of the salsa and garnish with lime wedges. Repeat with the remaining tortillas.

Prosciutto & Feta Pizza

Courtesy of Kimberly Wylie

Serves 2

INGREDIENTS:

¾ cup Warm Water (105 degrees)

1 ¼ tsp Dry Yeast

½ tsp Salt

1 ½ to 2 cups Flour

1 Tbsp + 1 tsp Olive Oil

1/4 Red Onion, thinly sliced

4 oz Grape Tomatoes, halved

2 Basil Leaves, thinly sliced

3 oz Sliced Prosciutto

1 Tbsp Honey

2 oz Fresh Mozzarella, sliced

1 oz Feta Cheese

Salt and Pepper to taste

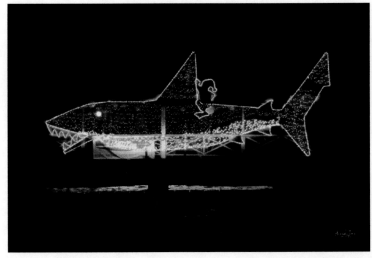

Photo by L. Kelly Jones

INSTRUCTIONS:

1. Mix water, yeast and salt in large mixing bowl or bowl of a stand mixer. Add just enough flour until dough comes together and is no longer sticky.

2. Knead either by hand or in stand mixer with dough hook, for 5 minutes. You're looking for a smooth and elastic dough.

3. Cover bowl with a clean dishtowel and place in a warm, draft-free area to rise 30 minutes. (In your oven, with just the oven light on, makes a perfect proofing temperature.)

4. Preheat oven to 400° F.

5. Heat 1 Tbsp olive oil in a medium pan over medium-high heat. Add onion to hot pan and sauté until translucent and just golden.

6. Add the honey and continue to cook until golden brown. Remove immediately from heat and place into a separate bowl, to ensure they don't burn from the residual heat in the pan.

7. Once all ingredients are prepared, it's time to build your pizza.

INSTRUCTIONS (cont.):

8. Remove your dough from the mixing bowl and roll out on a lightly-floured surface, into a 16-inch round crust. Alternately, you can hand stretch your pizza if you'd like.

9. Line a baking sheet with parchment paper or non-stick aluminum foil and place dough on the baking sheet.

10. Brush crust with 1 tsp olive oil. Season with a pinch of salt and pepper and top with toppings.

11. Bake pizzas until cheese is melted and crust is browned, approximately 10 to 15 minutes. Remove pizza from oven and let cool a few minutes before cutting.

TIPS:

- Storing your dry yeast in the freezer is the best way to keep it fresh.
- If your dough resists you too much when rolling out, let it rest for 5 minutes and try again.
- Roll each basil leaf lengthwise, into a long thin tube, then thinly slice each tube, to create nice, thin strips of basil.

Photo by L. Kelly Jones

Roasted Pork with Cranberry Glaze

Courtesy of Kimberly Wylie

INGREDIENTS:

4 to 5 lb Pork Loin

2 (14 oz) cans Whole Cranberry Sauce

1 cup Brown Sugar

½ tsp Ground Nutmeg

¼ tsp Salt

Pepper to taste

Olive Oil

Photo by Grant Wylie

INSTRUCTIONS:

1. Preheat oven to 350° F.

2. In a saucepan over medium-low heat combine cranberry sauce, brown sugar, nutmeg, salt, and pepper.

3. Continue to stir until well-blended and melted into a smooth glaze. Divide into two bowls, saving one for plating the roast when it's done.

4. Rinse roast and pat dry. (This is an important step.)

5. Place roast, fat side up, in the middle of a roasting pan.

6. Brush the roast with one bowl of cranberry glaze, including the ends.

7. Bake for 1 ½ to 2 hours, until internal temperature reaches 145° F.

8. Remove from oven and let roast 'rest' for fifteen minutes.

9. Slice into ¼-inch slices for serving and place on platter.

10. Drizzle remaining bowl of cranberry glaze over the slices.

Grilled Pork Tenderloin with Kiwi Salsa and Simple Salad

Courtesy of Kimberly Wylie

Serves 4

INGREDIENTS:

1 Kiwi, diced

2 oz. Pineapple, diced

1 Lime, zested and juiced

¼ oz. Cilantro, minced

1 ear Corn, shucked

1 Romaine Heart, coarsely chopped

1 lb Pork Tenderloin

½ tsp Salt

¼ tsp Black Pepper

1 tsp Olive Oil

1 oz. Mayonnaise

½ oz. Pepitas

INSTRUCTIONS:

1. Pat pork tenderloin dry and slice into tenderloin into medallions, ½"-¾" thick.

2. Season both sides with salt and pepper, and drizzle pork with 1 tsp olive oil.

3. Preheat grill over medium-high heat.

4. **To make the salsa:** combine kiwi, pineapple, 1 tsp lime juice, 1 tsp lime zest, and half the cilantro (reserve remaining for garnish) in a mixing bowl. Set aside to let flavors marry.

5. For the dressing, in another bowl, whisk together mayonnaise, 2 tsp water, 1 tsp lime juice, 1 tsp lime zest and a pinch of salt and pepper. Set aside.

6. Add corn to hot grill and cook until lightly charred, 2 to 3 minutes per side. Transfer to plate.

7. Add pork to grill and cook until browned and pork reaches a minimum internal temperature of 145° F, 3 to 4 minutes per side.

8. Transfer to a plate and rest 5 minutes. While pork rests, toss salad.

9. Once cool enough to handle, cut kernels from corn.

10. To bowl with dressing, add romaine and corn and combine. Season with ¼ tsp salt and a pinch of pepper and garnish with pepitas.

11. Place salad on plate alongside pork medallions. Spoon salsa over pork and garnish with remaining cilantro.

Dad's Delight

Courtesy of Vic Murphy of Vic's Karaoke Bar & Grill
Facebook.com/Vics-Karaoke-Bar-Grill-1170331026462508/

Serves 4

Just north of Grand Caribe, Vic's Karoake Bar & Grill is one of the funnest places to take your friends and sing your heart out. Great food, great drinks, and, if you're lucky, Elvis may come out and sing to you!

A note from Vic:

My father was Irish (with a name like Murphy, of course he was), and I grew up in the UK with my mum & dad, 3 brothers and 2 sisters. In addition to having no TV (hence so many kids), we didn't have a refrigerator. Yes we were fairly poor and so mum had to be strict and organized with the weekly food preparation. We knew ahead of time exactly what we would be eating for dinner every day, it was a sort of schedule and never changed. Many families were like that in the 1950s and 60s

So to Dad's Delight. I really don't know what it was called to be honest, but it was Dad's favorite, and I grew to love it too! It is very simple to cook and can be on the table from start to finish within 30 minutes. I still cook it today and have done so during this wretched quarantine - well, it's so easy!

INGREDIENTS:

4 lb Potatoes	1 pint Milk
1 (14.75 oz) tin of Pink Salmon	1 Egg
2 oz Corn Flour (starch)	2 oz Butter (divided)

Salt, Black Pepper and Rosemary Seeds to flavor.

INSTRUCTIONS:

1. Peel potatoes place in cold water and bring to the boil, then simmer for 20 minutes

2. Once cooked, drain and add 1 ounce butter, egg, teaspoon of black pepper, salt and rosemary and a splash of milk. Mash until creamy. Add the Salmon and continue to mash.

3. For the sauce, place the corn flour and a splash or two of cold milk into a saucepan and mix till smooth. Place on heat and add remaining 1 ounce of butter, a teaspoon of black pepper and the remainder of the milk stirring continuously until it boils.

4. Reduce heat and simmer for 3 minutes stirring occasionally.

5. Plate salmon & potato mash. Serve with vegetables of your choice (we always used garden peas) and add sauce to your liking. Enjoy!

Jambalaya

Courtesy of Terri Licht

Serves 12

INGREDIENTS:

½ lb Bacon, chopped

1 cup Onion, diced

1 cup Green Pepper, diced

1 cup Celery, diced

½ lb Smoked Sausage, diced

8 oz Chicken, boneless & diced

4 cups Beef Broth

4 cups Chicken Broth

2 cups Water

1 (15 oz) can Tomato Sauce

3 Roma Tomatoes, diced

2 tsp Cajun/Creole Seasoning

1 Tbsp Favorite Hot Sauce

1 tsp Salt

1 tsp Black Pepper

2 cups Uncooked Rice

2 Bay Leaves

6 Okra, sliced

20 Shrimp, peeled and deveined

INSTRUCTIONS:

1. In large stock pot, cook bacon until crispy. Remove bacon bits from the pot.

2. Brown the sausage and chicken in leftover bacon drippings.

3. Add onions, celery, green peppers and sauté until soft, 2 to 3 minutes.

4. Add remaining ingredients including bacon bits, minus rice, shrimp and okra and bring to a boil.

5. Add rice and okra and return to a boil. Cook for 20 minutes stirring frequently to keep rice from sticking.

6. During last 3 minutes, add shrimp and cook until pink.

7. Remove bay leaves and enjoy.

Hot lunches ready to go for
San Pedro Hot Lunch

Photo by Grant Wylie

DESSERTS

Apple Cake

Courtesy of Lucia Orndorff

INSTRUCTIONS:

1 ½ cups Wesson Oil

2 cups Sugar

3 Eggs

3 cups Flour

1 tsp Baking Soda

1 tsp Salt

2 tsp Ground Cinnamon

2 tsp Vanilla

3 cups Apples, chopped

1 cup Walnuts

Photo by Grant Wylie

INSTRUCTIONS:

1. Preheat oven to 325° F.

2. Mix this recipe well by hand. Do NOT use a mixer!

3. In a mixing bowl, combine oil, sugar and eggs.

4. Then add flour, baking soda, salt, cinnamon, vanilla, apples and walnuts and combine well.

5. Pour into a tube pan and bake for 1 ½ hours.

Remember - Do not use mixer!

Apricot Nectar Cake

Courtesy of Julie Kendall

INGREDIENTS:

1 box Duncan Hines Lemon Supreme Cake Mix

¾ cup Cooking Oil

½ cup Sugar

4 Eggs

1 (11 ½ oz) can Apricot Nectar (saving 1 Tbsp for glaze)

1 cup Powdered Sugar

½ stick Butter

¼ cup Lemon Juice

INSTRUCTIONS:

1. Preheat oven to 350º F.

2. Mix cake mix, oil, sugar, eggs, and most of apricot nectar in a bowl.

3. Bake in a greased & floured Bundt pan for 45 to 50 minutes until cooked through.

4. In a separate bowl, mix powdered sugar, lemon juice and 1 tablespoon nectar, to make glaze.

5. Pour over cake.

Cooking for San Pedro Hot Lunch

Preserved Peaches with Almonds

Courtesy of Chef Robin Halling - Private Chef, Restaurant Consultant, Head Chef
ChefRobinHalling.wixsite.com/mysite

Robin Halling is a gourmet chef who has worked in several Michelin star restaurants. Whether he's whipping up culinary masterpieces for visitors to Ambergris Caye, on a private yacht or in a luxury chalet, Robin's cuisine focuses on sustainable, locally-sourced ingredients that will delight your palate.

INGREDIENTS:

4 Peaches

200g Almonds, sliced

Thyme

1 pint Raspberries

300g Honey

3 Lemons

Ginger

200g Apple Juice

INSTRUCTIONS:

1. Cut peaches in half and fry them in a pan until golden.

2. Make a stock with honey, sliced ginger, lemon juice, and apple juice, by bringing to a boil and let cool down.

3. Vacuum pack or use a Mason jar to preserve your peaches with the stock syrup and let rest for 24 hours.

4. Assembly the peaches with sliced almonds on top and picked thyme leaves. Add your raspberries and a little of the stock syrup.

5. Goes well with vanilla ice cream or whipped vanilla cream.

Caramel Corn

Courtesy of Kimberly Wylie

INGREDIENTS:

24 cups Air-Popped Popcorn

1 cup Butter

1 cup Brown Sugar

¼ cup Light Corn Syrup

$^2/_3$ tsp Baking Soda

INSTRUCTIONS:

1. Preheat 200° F.

2. Mix butter, brown sugar and corn syrup in large sauce pan and bring to boil.

3. Remove from heat and add baking soda. This makes the caramel puff up BE SURE you have a pot large enough for this!

4. In batches, drizzle caramel over popcorn and toss to coat.

5. Spread on parchment paper-lined cookie sheets (I use 2 sheets.)

6. Cook for an hour, stirring 2 to 3 times.

7. Remove from oven and allow to cool, break into pieces and store in an airtight container.

TIP:

If you don't have an air popper, use two regular-sized plain bags of microwave popcorn

Swiss Cake Roll

Courtesy of Kimberly Wylie

This recipe can be served two ways — either simply dusted with confectioner's sugar once rolled or frosted.

FILLING INGREDIENTS:

2 cups Heavy Cream

½ cup Powdered Sugar

½ cup Unsweetened Cocoa Powder

1 tsp Vanilla Extract

CAKE INGREDIENTS (PART 1):

6 Egg Yolks

½ cup White Sugar

$1/3$ cup Unsweetened Cocoa Powder

1 tsp Vanilla Extract

$1/8$ tsp Salt

CAKE INGREDIENTS (PART 2):

6 Egg Whites

¼ cup White Sugar

FROSTING INGREDIENTS:

1 cup Salted Butter

½ cup Unsweetened Cocoa Powder

3 oz Semi-Sweet Chocolate, melted then cooled

½ tsp Instant Coffee

1 Tbsp Heavy Cream

3 ¼ cups Powdered Sugar

Powdered sugar for dusting

INSTRUCTIONS:

1. Preheat oven to 375° F and line a 10x15 inch jellyroll pan with parchment paper.

2. For the filling, in a large bowl, whip cream, 1/2 cup confectioners' sugar, 1/2 cup cocoa, and 1 teaspoon vanilla until thick and stiff and refrigerate.

3. In a separate large bowl, use an electric mixer to beat egg yolks with ½-cup sugar until thick and pale. Blend in $1/3$ –cup cocoa, 1 ½ teaspoons vanilla, and salt.

4. In another glass bowl, using clean beaters, whip egg whites to soft peaks. Gradually add ¼-cup sugar, and beat until whites form stiff peaks.

5. Immediately fold the yolk mixture into the whites. Spread the batter evenly into the prepared pan and bake for 12 to 15 minutes in the preheated oven.

6. Dust a clean dishtowel with confectioners' sugar and run a knife around the edge of the pan, and turn the warm cake out onto the towel. Remove and discard parchment paper.

7. Starting at the short edge of the cake, roll the cake up with the towel and cool for 30 minutes.

8. Unroll the cake, and spread the filling to within 1 inch of the ending rolled edge.

9. Re-roll the cake up with the filling inside. Place seam side down onto a serving plate, and refrigerate until serving.

10. Dust with confectioners' sugar before serving OR continue to make frosting as below.

11. **To make frosting:** melt chocolate in the microwave, slowly and carefully until liquid and smooth. Set aside to cool.

12. Whip the butter in your mixer until it's light and fluffy then add in the cocoa to the butter, beating until combined. Then when the chocolate is cool, add it to the butter mixture.

13. In a separate bowl, add the instant coffee to one tablespoon of cream, then add to butter mixture.

14. Add powdered sugar one cup at a time, beating until combined adjusting the thickness/texture by using a little more cream or slightly more confectioner's sugar, adding it slowly until the texture you want is achieved. Frost cake.

TIP:

- At Christmas time, BEFORE frosting, slice off 1/3 of the cooled roll at a 45-degree angle. Place this cut portion of the roll to the side of larger portion, angled end toward the larger piece to form a log-like structure. Run a fork over the frosting in lines.

Lockdown Lemon Zucchini Loaf

Courtesy of Susan Lala

INGREDIENTS:

1 ¼ cups Granulated Unprocessed Belizean Brown Sugar, large crystals if available otherwise regular white sugar

6 Tbsp Vegetable Oil

2 Eggs, room temperature

½ cup Water

2 Tbsp Lemon Juice

1 tsp Vanilla

2 cups White Flour

1 tsp Baking Soda

1 ½ cups Shredded Zucchini (do not squeeze)

INSTRUCTIONS

1. Preheat oven to 350° F.

2. Combine dry ingredients in one bowl and wet ingredients in a bowl large enough to comfortably hold all ingredients.

3. Then combine all saving the zucchini until the last.

4. Pour into a greased loaf pan.

5. Bake 35 to 40 minutes. A clean toothpick should come out a little gummy.

6. Cool before removing from pan.

Peanut Butter Pie

Courtesy of Jan Peo

This pie is so very easy and so very good! In just a few minutes you can have a delicious, decadent dessert literally whipped up.

INGREDIENTS:

4 oz Cream Cheese, softened to room temp

$1/_3$ cup Smooth Peanut Butter

1 (8 oz) container Cool Whip

1 cup Powdered Sugar

Crushed Peanuts

9" Graham Cracker Crust or 9' baked regular crust

INSTRUCTIONS:

1. With a mixer, combine cream cheese and peanut butter.

2. Blend in Cool Whip and sugar.

3. Pour into 9" pie crust and refrigerate for 4 hours.

4. Top with crushed peanuts.

Photo by L. Kelly Jones

Chocolate Delight

Courtesy of Julie Kendall

INGREDIENTS:

1 Cup flour

1 stick butter

1 Cup nuts

1 (8 oz) Cream Cheese

1 cup Powdered Sugar, sifted

1 (3.4 oz) Instant Vanilla Pie Filling

1 (3.4 oz) Instant Chocolate Pie Filling

2 cups Milk

1 (8 oz) tub Cool Whip

1 Hershey Candy Bar

INSTRUCTIONS:

1. Preheat oven to 325° F.

2. Blend together flour, butter and nuts, like a pie crust, and press into a 13 x 9 cake pan.

3. Bake 20 minutes.

4. Cool.

5. Cream together cream cheese and powdered sugar and spread over crust.

6. Combine vanilla and chocolate pie filling mixes with milk, with mixer on low speed for two minutes, and spread over cream cheese mixture.

7. Spread Cool Whip over chocolate mixture.

8. Grate Hershey candy bar and sprinkle over top.

Cinnamon Roll Dessert Pizza

Courtesy of Nancy Lindley

DOUGH INGREDIENTS:

1 ½ cups Warm Water

2 Tbsp Oil

2 Tbsp Sugar

1 Tbsp Yeast

3 ½ cups Flour

1 tsp Salt

DOUGH INSTRUCTIONS:

1. Mix warm water with sugar, sprinkle yeast over top and let react.

2. Mix flour and salt together in a large bowl

3. Once yeast is reacted, add oil to mixture, add yeast mixture to flour mixture. You may need to add a bit more flour. You should have a smooth and elastic dough that is tacky, but does not stick to your hands.

4. Knead for 5 to 8 minutes.

5. Roll out dough on a 12" greased pizza pan, let rise for 10 to 15 minutes.

CINNAMON SUGAR SPREAD INGREDIENTS:

2 Tbsp Soft margarine

½ cup Brown Sugar

½ cup Rolled Oats

½ tsp Cinnamon

CINNAMON SUGAR SPREAD INSTRUCTIONS:

1. Preheat oven to 425° F.

2. In a small bowl combine margarine, brown sugar, oats, and cinnamon. Spread thinly on top of the pizza crust.

3. Bake for 20 to 25 minutes or until the edges are lightly brown. After pizza is done, top with glaze.

GLAZE INGREDIENTS:

1 Tbsp Margarine

2 Tbsp Cream Cheese

¾ cup Icing Sugar

½ tsp Vanilla

GLAZE INSTRUCTIONS:

1. Beat together butter and cream cheese then add icing sugar and vanilla until combined

2. Drizzle over top of pizza.

Cheesecake Pumpkin Pie

Courtesy of Nancy Lindley

CRUST INGREDIENTS:

1 ½ cups Graham Crumbs

5 Tbsp Sugar

5 Tbsp Butter, melted

CRUST INSTRUCTIONS:

1. Preheat oven to 325° F.

2. Mix melted butter, sugar and graham crumbs together

3. Press firmly into the bottom of a large spring form pan

CHEESECAKE LAYER INGREDIENTS:

2 (8 oz) packages Cream Cheese, softened

½ cup White Sugar

½ tsp Vanilla Extract

2 Eggs

CHEESECAKE LAYER INSTRUCTIONS:

1. In a large bowl, combine cream cheese, sugar and vanilla. Beat until smooth.

2. Blend in eggs one at a time.

3. Spread into bottom of crust; set aside.

PUMPKIN PIE LAYER INGREDIENTS:

2 (8 oz) packages Cream Cheese, softened

1/2 cup White Sugar

1/2 tsp Vanilla Extract

2 Eggs

1 (15 oz) can Pumpkin Puree

½ tsp Ground Cinnamon

1 pinch Ground Cloves

1 pinch Ground Nutmeg

PUMPKIN PIE LAYER INSTRUCTIONS:

1. In a large bowl, combine cream cheese, sugar and vanilla. Beat until smooth.

2. Blend in eggs one at a time.

3. Add pumpkin (depending on how strong of a pumpkin flavor you would like, you can use ½ to a full small can of pumpkin puree), cinnamon, cloves and nutmeg to batter and stir gently until well blended.

4. Carefully spread over the cheese cake layer.

5. Bake in preheated oven for 45 to 50 minutes, or until center is almost set.

6. Allow to cool, then refrigerate for 3 hours or overnight.

7. Top with whipped cream if desire

Photo by Olivera Rusu at Cayo Espanto

Photo by Olivera Rusu
at Portofino Resort

by Oli
Olivera Rusu

BEVERAGES

Peanut Butter & Jelly Smoothie

Courtesy of Kimberly Wylie

Makes 2 servings

INGREDIENTS:

1 cup. Vanilla Almond Milk

1 cup. Strawberries

1 (5 to 6 oz) single-Serve. Strawberry Yogurt

4 Tbsp Creamy Peanut Butter

1 Tbsp Strawberry Preserves

2 cups Ice

INSTRUCTIONS:

1. Place all ingredients in blender, in the order above.

2. Blend until smooth

3. Divide between two glasses and enjoy!

Photo by Grant Wylie

Chocolate Strawberry Coconut Smoothie

Courtesy of Kimberly Wylie

Serves 2

INGREDIENTS:

8 oz. Strawberries

6 fl. oz. Coconut Milk

1 (5 to 6 oz) single serve. Vanilla Yogurt

1 fl. oz. Chocolate Syrup

2 cups Ice

INSTRUCTIONS:

1. Add all ingredients to blender in the order above.

2. Blend until smooth.

3. Divide into two glasses and enjoy!

S'mores Smoothie

Courtesy of Kimberly Wylie

Serves 2

INGREDIENTS:

3 oz. Marshmallow Fluff

1 fl. oz. Chocolate Syrup + more for glass rims

½ cup Graham Cracker Crumbs

8 fl. oz. Vanilla Almond Milk

1 (5 to 6 oz) single serve. Vanilla Greek Yogurt

2 cups Ice

INSTRUCTIONS:

1. Place small amount of chocolate syrup on a plate or shallow dish.

2. Place graham cracker crumbs on a second plate or shallow dish.

3. Coat the rims of two glasses by rolling in chocolate syrup.

4. Dip glass edge into graham cracker crumbs and set aside.

5. Place remaining ingredients into blender, in order of the above.

6. Blend until smooth.

7. Divide into rimmed glasses and enjoy!

Banana Cream Pie Smoothie

Courtesy of Kimberly Wylie

Serves 2

INGREDIENTS:

2 large Bananas

½ cup Low-Fat Vanilla Greek
 Yogurt

2 tsp Vanilla Extract

1 cup Milk

4 Vanilla Wafer Cookies

2 Tbsp Honey

¼ tsp Freshly Grated Nutmeg

½ tsp Ground Cinnamon

2 cups Ice

INSTRUCTIONS:

1. Place all ingredients in the body of a blender. Pulse until smooth and creamy.

2. Divide into two glasses and serve.

Photo courtesy of Rebecca Coutant author of
Fifty Big Experiences on Ambergris Caye, Belize
SanPedroScoop.com

Photo by Olivera Rusu
at Cayo Espanto

Special Thank You

Once again, I would like to thank you, the reader, for purchasing this book.

I would also like to once again thank everyone who contributed recipes and photos, as well as the Cypress Canyon Publishing team who donated their time to bring this book to life. Without you, this book couldn't have happened. Readers, please stop by the establishments who supported this project, when you come to visit us, and let them know you too appreciate their generosity.

Lastly, some have asked what will happen once the COVID pandemic is over and the San Pedro Hot Lunch program is no longer needed. This is a really great question!

Once the San Pedro Lunch Program is no longer providing hot meals to San Pedranos for free, the profits from this cookbook will be split between two longtime charity programs I also love on the island –

Hope Haven

and

The Babies and Elderly Pantry

Both of these charities are critical to those in need, on the island year-round.

Thank you, once again, and we hope to see you on Isla Bonita soon!

~ Kimberly Wylie

Photo by Olivera Rusu

Made in the USA
Coppell, TX
04 January 2022

70876461R00098